The Kids' Holiday Baking Book

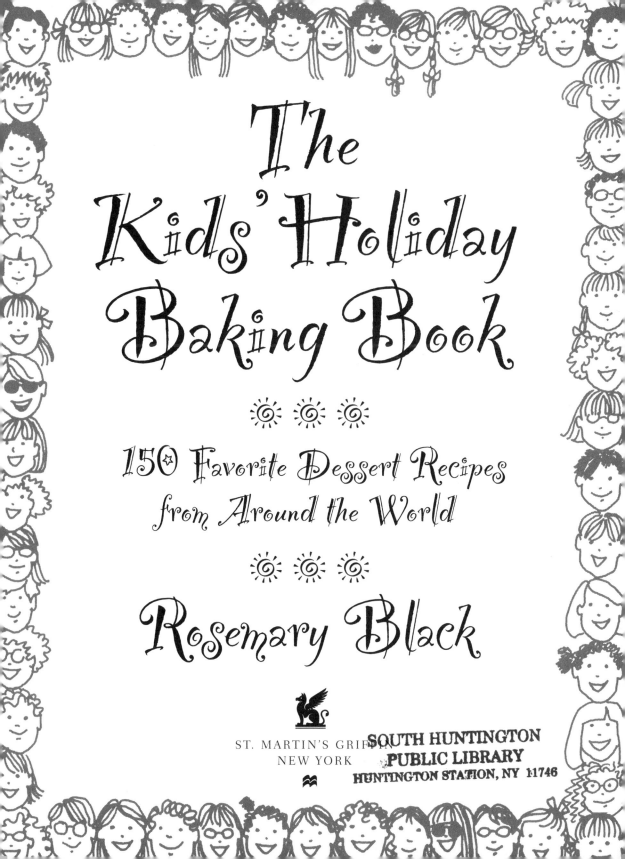

The Kids' Holiday Baking Book

※ ※ ※

150 Favorite Dessert Recipes from Around the World

※ ※ ※

Rosemary Black

ST. MARTIN'S GRIFFIN
NEW YORK

Illustrations copyright © 2003 by Durell Godfrey

www.stmartins.com

Library of Congress Cataloging-in-Publication Data

Black, Rosemary.
    The kids' holiday baking book : 150 favorite dessert recipes from around the world / Rosemary Black.
        p. cm.
    ISBN 0-312-31022-6
    1. Desserts. 2. Holiday cookery. 3. Cookery, International. I. Title.

TX773.B535 2003
614.8'6—dc21

                                                                2003046878

10 9 8 7 6 5 4 3

To my mother,
Dorothy Greene Black,
who taught me how to bake and how to live

Contents

Acknowledgments

Writing this book was pure joy for me because it involved my favorite activities: spending time with my kids, baking desserts, and eating sweets. It was also an incredible learning experience, as I researched unfamiliar holidays and tested and tasted cakes, pies, and cookies that I'd never even known existed. Of course, there were a few snafus along the way that tested my patience! My car that I was still making payments on was stolen, along with my only pair of eyeglasses, which came in handy for reading fine print. Four days later, lightning destroyed the hard drive on my computer and made me thank God that I'd backed up my half-finished book on disc. A few short months later, winter storms had me scrambling to rearrange the photo session for the cover. That the book came in right on deadline is due (in part) to my two decades of working as a reporter and editor for a big daily newspaper, where "late" is a very bad word. The other side was the wonderful family and friends who provided me with everything I needed, from a treasured recipe to a sympathetic ear. Without each and every one, this book wouldn't have been possible. My thanks go to:

Steve Lopez, my wonderful husband, for his unflagging support, computer expertise, and willingness to try each and every dessert in this book (and offer his comments with total honesty!).

My six wonderful children, Miranda, Molly, Karla, Kevin, Kerrie, and Madeline, for being my constant inspiration and source of energy, for testing recipes, and for always loving the desserts I've made for them through the years.

My precious father, Marcel Black, for his love, wisdom, sense of humor,

recipes, and for picking up the slack after the untimely death of my cherished mother, Dorothy Greene Black.

My father-in-law and mother-in-law, Dr. Robert and Marjorie Lopez, for their support, encouragement, and recipes.

My sisters and brothers, Chris Black, Maryellen Albanese, Janie Powers, Peggy Savage, Dorothy Barnes, Nancy Logan, Paul Black, Johnny Black, Barbara Price, and Betsy Black, for their memories and reminiscences, and special thanks to Dorothy Barnes and my sister-in-law, Joanne Black, for their help with the cover photograph, and to my nephew, Scott Black, and my nieces, Lauren and Rebecca Barnes, for appearing on the book cover, along with Kerrie and Madeline. My Aunt Puthie, Uncle Bob, Aunt Ginny, and Uncle Jim, for their memories and recipes.

My agent, Laura Williams, and her colleague, Martha Kaplan, for believing in this project right from the start, and my editor at St. Martin's, Marian Lizzi, for her patience and intuitive sense of what this book is about. And the other St. Martin's staffers for their help: Julie Mente, Shea Kornblum, Michael Storrings, Milenda Lee, and Jennifer Reeve, and to the illustrator, Durell Godfrey, and the photographer, Anthony Loew.

All my Pleasantville friends who contributed recipes, advice, and testing, in no particular order: Carol Lampert, Shari Applebaum (especially for letting us take photos for the cover in her kitchen), Sanda Krasnansky, Pat Eisemann, Lisa Friedman, Cathy Andreycak, Rosemary Carlough, Cathy Martyn, Sheri Xavier, and Regina Hogan.

My friends and colleagues who contributed recipes and advice, including Mila Andre, New York *Daily News* staffer and expert on Russian cookery; Nick Malgieri, author of many wonderful baking and Italian cookbooks; Julie Sahni, author of several excellent Indian cookbooks, Vandana Naik, pastry chef at Thom Restaurant, Doreen Novotny, Susan Waksman, Lenore Skenazy of the New York *Daily News*, Anjali Roye, Melissa Buyum and Zhao "Sunny" Zeng of the China Institute in Manhattan, and Karima Maloley of Al-Noor School in Brooklyn.

Introduction

A Year's Worth of Desserts for Special Occasions

Think back to some of your all-time favorite occasions. Chances are that many of the happiest times you remember center around holidays like Christmas, Chanukah, Thanksgiving, and Halloween. And however you celebrate these special occasions, a big part of the festivities is likely to involve dessert.

Maybe your family always decorates cookies together at Christmas, or you make a special honey cake for Rosh Hashanah. Just the aroma of a freshly baked pumpkin pie conjures up thoughts of a house spilling over with relatives who've gathered for Thanksgiving. And Halloween, the quintessential children's holiday, means parties, candy apples, popcorn balls, doughnuts, and cider.

Even though every month has at least one holiday that you probably look forward to each year, there are plenty of special occasions that kids in other parts of the world celebrate but that you may never have heard of! For instance, in Mexico, right around when we celebrate Halloween, children celebrate The Day of the Dead (*El día de los Muertos*) by eating a special sweet bread and candied pumpkin. In Italy, children observe St. Joseph's Day in March by feasting on delicious fried doughnuts.

On each of these special days, the kids in those countries eat traditional sweets that are lovingly prepared, year in and year out. In much the same way that you eat pumpkin pie for Thanksgiving, kids in other countries have particular desserts that they associate with special feast days.

Even on Christmas, kids around the world eat cookies that taste very different from the ones you're used to. In Germany, kids eat *pfeffernüsse*, which are little spicy drop cookies, and in Greece, they love *koulouria*, which are buttery little twists that are so tender they melt in your mouth.

In Cuba, children help make *buñuelos*, which are prepared with a vegetable called yucca and flavored with anise, a spice that tastes something like licorice.

Here in the United States, dessert is our favorite course. We always look forward to a sweet after eating the salad, main dish, and vegetables. Holiday desserts are fun to make and to eat, and I would love to show you how to make traditional cakes and cookies, pies and tarts, candies and custards, and creamy drinks that we enjoy on holidays. My own children (five girls and one boy) often bake desserts with me, and in this book, I've given recipes for all their favorites and more. While most of the recipes are for baked goods, I've chosen some that are chilled, or frozen, or that are ready right away—no oven needed!

I hope you enjoy learning about how children in faraway lands as well as right here in the United States celebrate holidays with sweets. I also hope not only that you will make holiday desserts with your family for the special days you celebrate, but that you start some new baking traditions at your house!

Just one more important note before you start cooking: This book isn't aimed only at kids, nor is it written for children of any specific age. Instead, my book is meant for parents and children to read and to use together. That's because cooking, besides being about good smells, wonderful tastes, and a means to satisfy us when we are hungry, is about being together and sharing a pleasurable activity with those we love. So enjoy, have fun, and let's eat dessert!

Getting Started

I f you want your desserts to look and taste great, be sure to read this chapter before you get started in the kitchen. You'll find all you need to know about equipment, utensils, and cooking terms, plus essential information about safety.

Equipment

BAKING PANS:
You'll use these to make cakes, muffins, cookies, cupcakes, and breads. The best sizes to keep on hand are two 9-inch round cake pans, one 9-inch square cake pan, a nine by five by three-inch loaf pan, two 12-cup muffin tins, two cookie sheets, one 9-inch pie pan, and a 9 by 13-inch cake pan.

CAKE PAN
SHEETCAKE
SQUARE PAN- GOOD FOR BROWNIES
LOAF PAN

COOKIE CUTTERS: Choose metal ones, which cut through dough more easily than plastic ones. It's fun to collect cookie cutters all year and keep them together in one large container for when you have a holiday baking extravaganza.

COOKIE CUTTERS FOR EVERY OCCASION

ELECTRIC MIXER: There are actually two different kinds: a super-sized one that has a built-in bowl and comes with a whip for beating egg whites and heavy cream, a hook for making dough for bread and rolls, and a paddle for cookie dough and cake batters; and a smaller handheld one that can be used in mixing bowls of various sizes and is a little bit easier for kids to use. With a small hand mixer, you really don't need a big one, although they're very nice for large jobs (when your mom and dad are on hand to help).

FOOD PROCESSOR: If there's one of these in your kitchen and you can get an adult to operate the machine, you can have shredded carrots and zucchini (for cakes) in seconds. It's also great for chopping nuts and chocolate, for pureeing mixtures, and for making pie crust. But it doesn't do everything. Don't try using it for whipping heavy cream or egg whites; you'll be disappointed.

DOUBLE BOILER: This funny-looking pan is actually two pans in one: The bottom part holds water, and the insert holds the food. It's useful for cooking foods, such as chocolate, that are very heat sensitive and must be exposed only to very low temperatures.

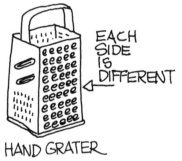

EACH SIDE IS DIFFERENT

HAND GRATER

GRATER: The four-sided one is best because it has different-size holes, from very fine to coarse. The coarse side is good for cheese; the finer sides are good for limes, lemons, and even fresh ginger.

MEASURING CUP

MEASURING CUPS: There are two different styles of measuring cups. One kind is used for measuring dry ingredients like flour and sugar. The most handy sizes of these to have are 1 cup, ½ cup, ⅓ cup, and ¼ cup. The measuring cups for

liquid ingredients often are made of glass and have a spout and a handle so you can easily pour out whatever you are measuring. The cups are marked in ounces and in fractions of cups.

MEASURING SPOONS: The set of four spoons that comes on a ring is handy because you can hang it from a little hook in the kitchen. A set usually has a tablespoon, a teaspoon, a ½ teaspoon, and a ¼ teaspoon.

MEASURING SPOONS

OVEN MITTS: If you take something out of a hot oven, slide one on each hand to avoid burns. And make sure you use a heavy one because the inside of an oven and the pans get very hot.

OVEN MITTS ARE VERY IMPORTANT

PARCHMENT PAPER: Sold by the roll in supermarkets, this is great for ensuring that your cookies don't stick to the baking sheets. You can also use it to line the bottoms of cake pans.

PASTRY BRUSH: Useful for buttering the tops of rolls and pastries, and for glazing cakes and cookies.

PASTRY BRUSH

ROLLING PIN: Made of wood or plastic, this gadget enables you to roll out pie dough and cookie dough with ease.

ROLLING PIN

ROTARY HAND BEATER: This versatile hand-operated mixer beats egg whites and whips heavy cream. After placing the beater part into the batter, hold the handle with one hand and crank the rotary handle with the other.

EGG BEATER

SAUCEPAN: A heavy one with a tightly fitting lid is essential. You'll use it to heat up milk or to boil water. If you have a nonstick one, you'll save yourself precious time when you're cleaning up.

SIFTER: A handy tool for thoroughly combining flour, sugar, salt, baking powder, and baking soda. Without a sifter, ingredients sometimes clump together, so it's definitely a worthwhile investment.

SPATULA: Wide rubber ones are great for mixing and for scraping out the bowl. With a narrow metal spatula, you can quickly remove cookies from the baking pan.

RUBBER SPATULA

WIRE RACKS: These are essential for cooling freshly baked cakes, cookies, and muffins, so keep several around.

WIRE WHISK: The small and medium ones are useful for beating eggs, stirring sauces, and mixing thin batters; large ones may be used for whipping cream.

WHISK

Cooking Terms

BAKE: To cook something, such as cakes, cookies, breads, or muffins, in the oven.

BEAT: To rapidly stir and mix ingredients, such as a batter or a dough, in order to incorporate air into the mixture. About 100 strokes by hand equals one minute with the electric mixer.

BOIL: To heat a liquid until bubbles appear and break on the surface.

CHOP: To cut up food into very tiny pieces. Put the food on the cutting board, position a sharp knife over it, and, holding the top (not sharp) of the blade with both hands, rock the knife up and down over the food.

CREAM: To combine butter and sugar and beat until fluffy. A creamed mixture should be nice and light before you add other ingredients.

CUT IN: To use a pastry blender or two knives to incorporate butter or shortening into flour. Often a recipe will say to cut in the butter until it is the consistency of peas or cornmeal.

DICE: To cut food into small square pieces, using a sharp knife. Diced vegetables are typically in pieces that are about ¼ inch square.

DUST: To sprinkle sugar, flour, or cocoa powder over a food, using a sifter.

FOLD: To very gently combine a light mixture (such as beaten egg whites) with a heavier mixture, such as a custard. Use a rubber spatula to cut into the two mixtures, reaching to the bottom of the bowl, and then bring the spatula back up. Rotate the bowl a quarter turn each time you bring the spatula back up to the top of the bowl so that the two mixtures become well combined.

GLAZE: To use a knife to coat muffins and cakes with a thin icing.

GREASE: To spread a little butter, shortening, or margarine around the bottom and sides of a pan in order to prevent cakes or cookies from sticking.

KNEAD: To work the dough, with your hands, with the dough hook of an electric mixer, or in a food processor. A well-kneaded dough is smooth and elastic.

ROLL OUT: To make a ball of dough very thin for a pie crust, place it on a floured work surface and use a rolling pin to make strokes in all directions so that the dough thins out evenly.

SCALD: To bring a liquid such as milk just to a boil, or until a film begins to form on the surface.

SEPARATE EGGS:
The easiest way to do this is to gently tap the egg against the edge of a little dish. Hold the egg over

the dish and gently open the crack, allowing the white to fall into the dish. Pull your hands apart a little and let the egg shell split in half. The yolk should be in one of these halves. You don't want to have any egg yolks in the bowl if you are planning to whip whites for a meringue because the whites won't whip up to as great a volume as is necessary for a really fluffy meringue.

SIFT: To remove any lumps from dry ingredients by passing them through a sifter or sieve into a mixing bowl or onto waxed paper.

TEST FOR DONENESS: To insert a cake tester into the middle of a cake; if it emerges clean, the cake is done.

WHIP: To beat ingredients in order to incorporate air into them and to make them light and fluffy.

Ingredients

BAKING POWDER: A white powder that is a leavener, meaning it's used to lighten batters and dough. Buy the one that says "double-acting."

BAKING SODA: Also a white powder, this leavener must be combined with an acid like sour cream or buttermilk, and sometimes with baking powder, to make it work.

BUTTER: The best butter for baking is "sweet," or unsalted, butter, but it doesn't make a tremendous amount of difference, so use whichever you have on hand.

CARDAMOM: Very aromatic, this spice is native to India but grows in other tropical areas, too. The seeds come in small pods that are only about as large as a blueberry. The pods can contain up to twenty seeds. When a recipe calls for cardamom seeds, you will need to remove the seeds from the pods, and then discard the pods. Sometimes a recipe will call for ground cardamom, and then you can just measure it out. But remember, a little goes a long way when you are cooking with this spicy-sweet ingredient.

CHOCOLATE: Unsweetened chocolate, sometimes called baking or bitter chocolate, has chocolate liquor and between 50 and 58 percent cocoa butter. Bittersweet chocolate has at least 35 percent chocolate liquor, while semisweet chocolate and sweet chocolate have between

15 and 35 percent chocolate liquor. When dry milk is added to sweetened chocolate, milk chocolate is the result. You can use bittersweet, semisweet, and sweet chocolate interchangeably in some recipes, but milk chocolate (because of the milk protein) shouldn't be substituted for one of these. White chocolate, believe it or not, isn't chocolate at all. Instead, it's made with sugar, cocoa butter, milk solids, lecithin, and vanilla.

CINNAMON: You have probably eaten cinnamon toast and cinnamon rolls, but have you ever seen a cinnamon stick? Reddish brown in color, it comes from the inner bark of a tropical evergreen tree. The bark is dried, and then sold as sticks or ground into a powder.

COCONUT MILK: This liquid is prepared by simmering equal parts water and shredded fresh coconut meat, then straining it through a cheesecloth. Although it is tricky to make, you can now buy canned coconut milk in Asian markets and in some supermarkets. It's different from cream of coconut, which is richer and very sweet. Cream of coconut, which also comes in a can, is an ingredient in some desserts and drinks.

CORNSTARCH: Yet another white powder, this one is used as a thickener. Typically, it needs to be dissolved in a little cold water before it is added to a liquid and then brought to a boil.

EGGS: All eggs are graded according to their size, and the recipes in this book all use extra-large eggs. There isn't any difference in taste between white and brown eggs so use whichever you like. Any egg that's cracked when you take it out of the package should be discarded. Because of the slight risk of foodborne illness that raw eggs can pose, they aren't used in any of these recipes.

FLOUR: Made from very finely ground meal from various grains, typically wheat. Wheat flour contains gluten, a protein that helps dough or batter to rise, develop flavor, and expand. Most of the recipes in this book call for all-purpose flour, which is made from a mixture of hard winter wheat and soft spring wheat, with a gluten content that is in the middle. Cake flour, which is made from soft wheat, has a low gluten content. Self-rising flour already has baking powder and salt added to it. Whole-wheat flour, which is made from the whole grain, has more nutrients than white flour and has a nice nutty flavor.

NUTMEG: It's native to the Spice Islands and grows on a tree. The little egg-shaped nutmeg, which is revealed once the fruit of the tree is picked and split, has a warm and spicy aroma. You can buy it either ground or whole. Grind your own with a little nutmeg grater if you want the best flavor in your puddings, cookies, and pies.

OIL: There are many kinds, each with its own taste. Vegetable oils include corn, peanut, safflower, and soybean. They can withstand high heat so are good for cooking. Olive oil is more expensive and so should be used sparingly. It's not good for deep frying because it burns more quickly than some oils. Peanut oil has a faintly peanutty taste that enhances the flavor of some dishes.

RICE FLOUR: This fine, powdery flour, made from regular white rice, is used in a lot of Chinese baked goods. You can also find another kind, called glutinous rice flour, or sweet rice flour, which is made from a high-starch, short-grain rice. Besides being used in desserts, glutinous rice flour thickens sauces.

RICE VINEGAR: Made from fermented rice, this vinegar has a slightly milder flavor than the regular wine or cider variety. It is found in Asian markets and in the ethnic food aisle of many supermarkets.

ROLLED OATS: The best kind to use in muffins and cookies are the quick-cooking oats. Avoid using prepackaged instant oatmeal in baked goods.

ROSE WATER: Used in Indian cooking and in Chinese cooking, this flavoring is made from rose petals and is very fragrant. In fact, it almost smells like rose perfume. Just a little goes a very long way.

SAFFRON: The world's most expensive spice, it's got a pungent, unique flavor. It's made from the stigmas of the purple crocus.

SEMOLINA: This is durum wheat that has been ground more coarsely than other wheat flours. It is used to make homemade pasta and puddings and other desserts.

SUGAR: Sure, they're all sweet, but some kinds are sweeter than others, and they each affect a dish in a different way, so be sure to use the one the recipe calls for. Granulated sugar is ordinary table sugar, the kind you sprinkle on cereal. Confectioners' sugar, or powdered sugar, is fine granulated sugar that has a little cornstarch in it to make it powdery. It's used for frostings and for sprinkling on cookies and other baked goods. Brown sugar has molasses added to it. The dark brown variety has a richer taste and has more molasses in it than light brown, which is more commonly used in desserts. Avoid granulated brown sugar in baked goods because it yields disappointing results.

VEGETABLE SHORTENING: A creamy white solid substance that comes in a can and in foil-wrapped sticks, it's used for making pie crusts and for frying, and it lasts for a very long time on the pantry shelf without refrigeration.

YEAST: A leavening agent used in breads and rolls, it needs sugar and starch, plus a liquid, to work. The little foil packages of yeast sold in the supermarkets last for several months in the cupboard. Check the expiration date and discard the yeast if it has expired.

Safety Tips

- Before starting to cook, wash your hands with warm, soapy water and rinse and dry them thoroughly. Wash them again after handling food. Don't put your hands near your nose or mouth while cooking.
- Wear comfortable old clothes when you cook, but make sure that your sleeves aren't long or baggy and that your hair isn't hanging down into your face. These could catch on fire or get caught in an appliance like a beater. Wear an apron to protect your clothing.

- Read the recipe through completely before starting to cook, and review it with a grown-up to see if you will need help from him or her.
- Prepare foods on a clean work surface, using clean utensils. Wash all fruits with cold running water before using.
- If you are old enough to use a knife, always hold it by the handle, never by the blade. And concentrate when you are cutting with a knife. Don't get distracted, because that's when accidents happen.
- As you cut, make sure the sharp edge of the blade is facing straight down toward the food you're cutting. Grip the handle with all the fingers of one hand and hold your thumb firmly against the handle's other side. Use your other hand as a guide; let it hold the food being cut firmly on the board, and keep

the fingers on this hand positioned so that the fingertips are curled back and the thumb is out of the way of the knife as it holds down the food.

- Never put a dirty knife in a sink full of dishes, where it can be hard to spot. Wash the knife separately, dry it, and put it away.
- When walking with a knife, hold it by the handle with the point of the blade facing down. If you are old enough to use a peeler, always hold it very firmly in your hand. Move it away from you as you peel the skin from the fruit or vegetable.
- If you use a grater, be careful so that you don't scrape your fingers or knuckles on the rough holes.
- Keep cold foods cold and hot foods hot. If a food that is meant to be served hot or cold is left at room temperature for more than two hours, discard it.
- Keep pot holders and oven mitts close at hand while you are cooking. They will protect your hands from anything hot that you pick up. Get in the habit of picking up a pot holder or mitt before you pick up a hot pot or pan. You also should use one when you slide baking pans in or out of the oven.
- Be very careful around stove burners and keep in mind that the heat from the burners can make the rest of the stove hot. Keep pot and pan handles turned toward the center of the stove so that no one will accidentally bump into the handle and spill the hot contents.
- After you eat, refrigerate or freeze perishable foods quickly.

New Year's Eve and New Year's Day

If your parents let you stay up late on New Year's Eve, chances are that you all turn on the TV to watch the descent of the giant ball in New York's Times Square. Just at midnight, it seems to pick up speed, and the countdown moves ever more quickly toward the final moments of the old year. Finally, officially, it's the New Year on TV and at home, and everyone blows noisemakers, throws confetti, and kisses one another. The grown-ups have a champagne toast, and kids get all kinds of goodies to eat.

New Year's observances have been under way for thousands of years, though not always on January 1. The origins of the celebration can be traced back four thousand years to the Babylonians, who held a big festival each spring to mark the next cycle of planting and harvest.

The beginning of spring is actually a logical time for New Year's parties, since it is the season of rebirth and of planting new crops. The Romans were in the habit of observing the New Year in late March, but various emperors were constantly tampering with the calendar.

January 1 wasn't established as the first day of the year until 46 B.C. When Roman Emperor Julius Caesar established his own calendar that year, he chose the date of January 1. Ever since then, we've been operating on this calendar, called the Julian calendar, after Caesar.

As for the word *January*, it comes from the Romans, who named the month for their god, Janus; he is pictured with two heads. One looks forward, and the other looks back, to symbolize a break between the old and the new.

In the first centuries A.D., the New Year was celebrated by the Romans, but the early Catholic Church frowned on the festivities.

Still, as Christianity spread, the early church began planning its own religious observances.

As New Year's festivities became more widespread, people thought that they could affect the outcome of the coming year by what they did or ate on the very first day of the year. So it became typical for people to celebrate the first few minutes of the new year with family and friends, often hosting parties into the middle of the night.

All around the world, various nations welcome the New Year with their own traditions. In Japan, families may hang a rope of straw across the front of their houses to keep out evil spirits and bring good luck and happiness. In Scotland, friends and relatives visit one another. They believe that if your first visitor on New Year's Eve is a man with dark hair or dark skin, then you'll have prosperity in the new year. People in Scotland eat shortbread, oatmeal cake, a bread made with currants, and delicious biscuitlike pastries called "scones."

French people celebrate New Year's by throwing a family dinner party and exchanging presents and greeting cards. They like to eat a sweet bread called "brioche," plus chocolates and other sweets. Cuban families have a unique New Year's tradition: They eat twelve grapes, one for every stroke of midnight. Near the stroke of midnight, everyone in the family counts out a dozen grapes into their glass. Just when the clock strikes midnight, all raise their glasses, say "Salud!" and try to eat the grapes before a minute is up. This toast is thought to bring good luck in the coming year.

Traditional New Year's foods are believed to bring luck. In some countries, people believe that any ring-shaped food is good luck because it symbolizes "coming full circle," and completing a year's cycle. In Holland, for example, people believe that eating doughnuts on New Year's Day will bring them good fortune.

Of course, a big part of New Year's celebration is making resolutions. When I was growing up, each New Year's Eve I would write down all the ways that I planned to improve myself in the coming year, from studying harder to being kinder to my younger brothers and sis-

ters. And at the beginning of each year, when I was highly motivated, I actually stuck to them. By the time New Year's Eve rolled around again, though, many of my resolutions had fallen by the wayside. But of course I was always filled with determination that the next year, I'd be a better person.

Dutch Doughnuts

(Oliebollen)

Traditionally, doughnuts are fried, but frying can be dangerous for kids. These doughnuts are oven-baked so they are easier to make. Eat one for good luck in the New Year!

1½ cups milk
⅓ cup vegetable shortening
3 tablespoons granulated sugar
3 tablespoons brown sugar
2 packages active dry yeast
⅓ cup warm water
2 teaspoons salt
1½ teaspoons ground nutmeg
2 eggs
4½ to 5½ cups all-purpose flour plus extra for the work surface and rolling pin
Vegetable shortening for greasing the pan

For the coating:
¼ cup (½ stick) butter
¾ cup sugar
½ teaspoon ground cinnamon

1. In a medium saucepan, heat the milk over low heat. When it is very warm, add the vegetable shortening and stir until it has melted. Add the granulated sugar and brown sugar and stir well. Remove the pan from the heat and let the mixture cool to room temperature.

2. In a large mixing bowl, stir the yeast into the warm water until it has dissolved. When the milk mixture is room temperature, pour it over the water-yeast mixture. Add the salt and the nutmeg.

3. In a small bowl, lightly beat the eggs with a whisk or fork. Add the beaten eggs to the yeast mixture. Stir in 2 cups of the flour. Beat and stir with a large spoon until a dough begins to form. Add 1 more cup of flour and stir again. Add 1½ more cups and stir with the spoon until the dough is smooth. Add more flour as needed so the dough isn't too sticky. Cover the bowl with a damp clean towel and allow the dough to rise for about 1 hour or until it has doubled in size.

4. Preheat the oven to 450°F. Lightly grease 2 baking sheets. Dust a clean work surface with flour. Turn the dough out onto the work surface. Dust a rolling pin with flour and roll out the dough into a big circle that is about ½ inch thick, occasionally dusting the dough

with flour so it won't stick. With a 3-inch doughnut cutter, cut out doughnuts. Carefully lift the doughnuts off the work surface and place them about 1 inch apart on the baking sheets. Continue to cut out doughnuts and place them on the baking sheets. Allow the doughnuts to rise for about 20 minutes.

5. Bake the doughnuts for about 10 minutes or until the tops are golden. While the doughnuts are baking, ball up the leftover dough scraps, roll out, and cut out more doughnuts. Remove the baked doughnuts from the oven and let them cool on a wire rack. Allow the unbaked doughnuts to rise for 20 minutes. Place them in the oven and bake for 10 minutes or until done.

6. In a small saucepan, heat the butter over low heat until it has melted. Allow the melted butter to cool. Place the sugar and the cinnamon in a paper bag. With a pastry brush, brush the doughnuts with the melted butter. Gently shake them in the cinnamon-sugar mixture. Eat while warm. You can also freeze these doughnuts and reheat them later on.

Scottish Scones

MAKES 1 DOZEN

I think you'll agree with the Scottish that scones taste great anytime. Try these warm for breakfast, spread with strawberry jam.

2 cups all-purpose flour
2½ teaspoons baking powder
3 tablespoons sugar
1 teaspoon salt
¼ cup vegetable shortening, such as Crisco
½ cup milk
1 egg
Flour for the work surface and your hands

For the topping:
3 tablespoons milk
3 tablespoons sugar

1. Preheat the oven to 450°F. Into a large mixing bowl, sift the flour, baking powder, sugar, and salt. Add the vegetable shortening and rub it in, using your fingertips, until the mixture has the consistency of peas. Stir in the milk.

2. In a small cup, lightly beat the egg. Add it to the dough. Mix just until the flour mixture is moistened. Form the dough into a ball and press the edges together.

3. Lightly dust a work surface with flour and turn out the dough onto the work surface. Use the heel of your hands to knead the dough for about 2 minutes. To do this, first flour your hands. Then, gather the dough together. Use the heel of one hand to push the top part of the dough away from you. Then fold this piece over the dough that is closest to you. Turn the dough a quarter turn, clockwise, and repeat. You should knead the dough till it's smooth, not sticky. With your fingers, pat the dough into a big circle that is about ½ inch thick.

KNEAD DOUGH

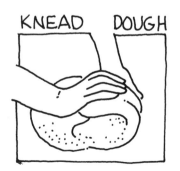

4. With a pastry brush, brush 3 tablespoons of the milk over the dough and sprinkle it with the 3 tablespoons of sugar. Cut the circle of dough into 12 pie-shaped wedges. Place them about 1 inch apart on an ungreased baking sheet.

5. Bake for 10 to 13 minutes, until the tops are golden brown. With a spatula, remove the scones to a wire rack to finish cooling.

Variation: You may stir either ½ cup mini chocolate chips or ½ cup raisins into the dough after adding the egg and before pressing the dough into the shape of a ball.

Almond Shortbread

In Scotland it's considered very lucky if a household's first visitor of the year is male, dark-haired, and comes bearing shortbread. Here's a delicious variation on plain shortbread. Even if it's not served by a dark, handsome chef, it's wonderful. This recipe is adapted from one that ran in the New York Daily News, *December 26, 1979.*

2 cups all-purpose flour
¾ cup (1½ sticks) unsalted butter, at room temperature
¾ cup sugar
1½ teaspoons baking powder
Pinch of salt
3 eggs (2 of them separated)
3½ ounces almond paste (½ of a 7-ounce package)
1 teaspoon water
1 teaspoon ground cinnamon

1. Preheat the oven to 325°F. In a large mixing bowl, sift the flour over the butter. Beat with an electric mixer set on medium speed for 2 minutes. Add the sugar, baking powder, and salt; beat well. Add the whole egg and 2 egg yolks, reserving the egg whites.

2. Knead the mixture with your hands for about 5 minutes or until well mixed and springy. Press into an 8-inch round cake pan, reserving about ⅓ of the dough.

3. In a small bowl, combine the almond paste with the water and cinnamon. Mix well to form a smooth paste. In a medium bowl, beat the reserved 2 egg whites until stiff. Fold the beaten egg whites into the almond paste mixture. Spread the mixture over the dough in the cake pan.

4. With a rolling pin, roll the reserved dough into strips and press into the almond mixture to form a crisscross design.

5. Bake for 45 minutes or until a toothpick inserted into the center comes out clean. Cut into wedges. Serve warm or at room temperature.

Fizzy and Festive New Year's Punch

While the grown-ups are sipping champagne, the kids can hoist a toast to the new year with this sparkling beverage. It's nice to serve it in a big punch bowl, but you could just as easily pour it out of a large pitcher.

1 quart very hot water
1¼ cups superfine sugar
1 quart cranberry-apple juice
Juice of 1 lemon
2 cups orange juice (the no-pulp kind)
1 quart ginger ale

1. In a large pot, stir the hot water and the sugar until the sugar has dissolved. Add the remaining ingredients except for the ginger ale. Refrigerate until chilled.

2. Just before serving, add the ginger ale and pour over ice into a pitcher or a punch bowl.

New Year's Eve and New Year's Day **21**

Frosty Snowmen

SERVES 4

This is half punch and half dessert. Serve it in tall glasses with a straw.

2 (10-ounce) packages
frozen strawberries,
partially thawed
1 cup very cold water
2 cups orange juice
4 large scoops vanilla ice
cream
4 orange slices

1. In a blender, combine the strawberries, water, and orange juice. Blend on medium speed for 45 seconds or until smooth. Pour into 4 glasses.

2. Float 1 scoop of ice cream in each. Garnish each serving with an orange slice. Serve immediately.

Loaded with Chips
Cream Cheese Pound Cake

My children call this favorite dessert Mom's Cake. It is a recipe that I copied out of my mother-in-law's recipe files years ago, and it is definitely a keeper. It's versatile—you can substitute chopped nuts or raisins for the mini chocolate chips—and I always make it at New Year's.

Vegetable shortening for greasing the pan

1 (8-ounce) package cream cheese, at room temperature

1 cup (2 sticks) butter, at room temperature

1½ cups sugar

1½ teaspoons vanilla extract

4 eggs

2¼ cups sifted all-purpose flour

1½ teaspoons baking powder

¾ cup mini chocolate chips

BUNDT PAN

1. Preheat the oven to 325°F. Lightly grease a 12-cup Bundt pan or tube pan.

2. In a large mixing bowl, with an electric mixer on medium speed, beat the cream cheese, butter, sugar, and vanilla for 2 minutes. Add the eggs, one at a time, beating well after each addition.

3. Into a medium bowl, sift 2 cups of the flour with the baking powder. Add the flour mixture gradually to the butter mixture and beat well after each addition.

4. In a small bowl, stir the remaining ¼ cup flour and the chocolate chips. Fold this into the batter.

5. Spoon and scrape the batter into the prepared pan. Level the top. Bake for 55 to 65 minutes or until a cake tester inserted into the center of the pan comes out clean. Cool in the pan for 10 minutes. Loosen the edges of the cake with a knife. Invert the cake onto a serving platter and allow it to cool completely.

Canadian Butter Tarts

Since many relatives on my father's side of the family live in Canada, we visited there from time to time when I was growing up. I always thought back then (and still do) that Canadians have the most wonderful desserts. My favorite has always been butter tarts, which were first introduced to me by my Auntie Mary Flanagan, who lived in Toronto. The name might sound kind of weird, but these rich pastries are incredibly delicious. You wouldn't want to eat them every day since they are high in fat and sugar, but on New Year's, everyone deserves to splurge. If you like, substitute currants for the raisins, and feel free to add some chopped nuts, too.

For the pastry:
- 2 cups all-purpose flour plus extra for the work surface
- 1 teaspoon salt
- ¾ cup vegetable shortening
- 5 to 7 tablespoons ice water

1. Preheat the oven to 450°F.

2. *Make the pastry:* Into a large bowl, sift the flour and the salt. Blend in the shortening and crumble it with your fingers until the particles are the size of small peas. Add 5 tablespoons water and mix with a fork. Add 1 or 2 more tablespoons water, if necessary, so dough clumps together. Knead the dough slightly with your hands to form a smooth ball.

3. On a lightly floured work surface, roll out the dough to about a ½-inch thickness. Cut it with a sharp knife to fit into 8 small (3- or 4-inch) tart pans. Fit the dough into the pans.

For the filling:
1/2 cup (1 stick) unsalted butter
2 eggs
2 cups firmly packed brown sugar
2 tablespoons white vinegar
1 tablespoon vanilla extract
1/2 cup raisins, optional

For the topping:
1/2 cup heavy cream
4 tablespoons sugar

4. *Make the filling:* In a small glass bowl, melt the butter in the microwave. Set it aside to cool. In a medium bowl, lightly beat the eggs with a whisk. Beat in the brown sugar, vinegar, vanilla, cooled butter, and raisins (if using). Fill the tart shells about 2/3 full.

5. Bake the tarts for 7 minutes. Reduce the heat to 325°F and bake for about 10–15 minutes longer. Remove from the oven when the filling is just set. Watch carefully so the tarts don't burn! Cool on a rack.

6. *Make the topping:* In a medium bowl, with an electric mixer set on high speed, beat the heavy cream until soft peaks form. Gradually add the sugar and beat until stiff peaks form. Spread the whipped cream over the cooled tarts. Store leftover tarts in the refrigerator, and eat within one day.

Epiphany

There's a terrible letdown feeling that settles in at the end of December, with Christmas over for another whole endless year and school looming in just a few more days. But in many areas of the world, right after Christmas, children are celebrating another holiday, Epiphany or Three Kings Day. Known in many countries as *El día de los reyes,* the holiday, which falls on January 6, celebrates the divinity of Christ and is an occasion to recognize Jesus as the redeemer.

For Christians, the day marks the arrival of the three wise men (Balthazar, Gaspar, and Melchior), who more than two thousand years ago traveled to Bethlehem bearing gifts of gold, frankincense, and myrrh for the Christ Child.

In Puerto Rican and Cuban families, Epiphany is a holiday that focuses especially on children. Latino kids sing holiday songs, and they decorate and fill a shoebox with grass for the camels. They often use the same shoebox year after year, and they may write a letter to the three kings and attach it to the box. Children leave out a bowl of water for the thirsty camels, and just as Santa Claus leaves behind an empty milk glass and an empty cookie plate in homes where thoughtful youngsters leave him a snack, there's likely to be an empty water bowl and some missing grass when the children wake up! Some kids also set out drinks, cookies, or nougat for the three kings.

In Spain, grown-ups dress up as the three wise men and sail into Barcelona the day before the Epiphany. Some of these boats are stocked with candy, which the costumed sailors toss into the crowd of viewers. One boat also carries coal as a reminder for children to be good! In Spanish homes, shoes, rather than stockings, are set out in the living room, and in the morning, children find them piled up with gifts and topped with a sweet treat.

The sweets on Epiphany are especially tempting and vary from country to country. In Puerto Rico on this holiday as well as on Christmas, children feast on a coconut rice pudding that is served chilled and sprinkled with cinnamon. In Germany, families serve sweets with coffee or tea each day from Christmas right on through Epiphany, and the German cookies are especially wonderful. German cooks often begin to make pepper nuts, a spicy cookie, in November because they taste best after they have ripened in tins for several weeks.

In Oaxaca, Mexico, on the afternoon of Three Kings Day, children drink a special chocolate beverage. In Puerto Rico, children eat a feast and drink *coquito*, which is a coconut eggnog.

In many countries, including Mexico and Spain, a traditional Three Kings cake is actually a bread shaped like a wreath. Called *rosca de reyes*, it's coated with sugar, candied fruit, and slivered almonds. The bread is baked with a dried bean or a little doll inside. When it is sliced, the platter is covered with a napkin and spun around. Everyone chooses a slice at random, and the lucky person who finds the bean or the doll is crowned "Bean King" for the coming year.

Russians celebrate Christmas on Three Kings Day, and there is gift giving, feasting, and plenty of sweets. Children love to eat *blinchiki*, which are paper-thin pancakes that may be filled with fruits or preserves, or dusted with confectioners' sugar and served with sour cream, or rolled into tubes and stuffed with applesauce.

Cinnamon-Topped Coconut Rice Pudding from Puerto Rico

SERVES 8–12

Puerto Rican children love this cinnamon-topped pudding. It's cool and creamy, and you can eat it for breakfast or for dessert. When you are shopping for coconut milk, check out ethnic food stores or the ethnic products aisle of the supermarket. Be sure you get coconut milk, and not coconut cream, which is a sweet product used in many mixed drinks. This tastes best the day it's made.

5½ cups canned coconut milk
1 cup uncooked rice
¾ teaspoon salt
¼ teaspoon ground ginger
¾ teaspoon ground cinnamon plus more for sprinkling on top
½ teaspoon ground cloves
⅓ cup raisins, optional
1 cup sugar

1. In the top of a large double boiler over simmering water, bring 4 cups of the coconut milk to a boil. Stir in the rice, salt, ginger, ¾ teaspoon of the cinnamon, and the cloves. Cover and cook over very low heat for 45 minutes to 1 hour, stirring every 5 minutes or so, until the rice is tender and the pudding is thick. Gradually add ½ cup coconut milk only if the pudding starts to look dry.

2. At the end of the hour, stir the remaining cup of coconut milk, the raisins, and the sugar. Cook for another 15 minutes or until the pudding is very creamy.

3. Pour the pudding into a pretty glass serving bowl, cover with plastic wrap, and refrigerate. Just before you serve it, sprinkle with more cinnamon. You can also top the pudding with whipped cream.

Coquito

(Puerto Rican Eggnog)

A delicious drink that Puerto Rican children look forward to on Three Kings Day. Be sure to buy canned sweetened condensed milk, not canned evaporated milk.

3 cups packaged
   unsweetened shredded
   coconut
I cup hot water
I cup sweetened
   condensed milk
1½ cups chilled egg nog
   (store-bought)
Ground cinnamon for
   the topping

1. In a large mixing bowl, place the coconut. Add the hot water. Stir and let steep for 10 minutes.

2. Strain the liquid into the blender. Arrange a paper coffee filter in a strainer and set the strainer over a bowl. Put the coconut pulp into the coffee filter. Squeeze and press on the pulp to extract as much of the liquid as possible. Add whatever liquid drips into the bowl to the coconut milk in the blender. Discard the coconut pulp.

3. Add to the blender the condensed milk and the chilled egg nog. Blend on high speed for 45 seconds.

4. Transfer the beverage to a pitcher; cover and refrigerate for at least 2 hours. When ready to serve, ladle into glasses and sprinkle with cinnamon.

Fit for Royalty
Three Kings Cake

Serve this cakelike bread for breakfast—it is fit for a king!

3 or more cups
  all-purpose flour
I envelope active dry
  yeast
½ cup plus I tablespoon
  milk
½ cup granulated sugar
¼ cup (I stick) cold
  butter, cut into pieces,
  plus extra for greasing
  the dough
I teaspoon salt
I whole egg and
  I egg yolk, beaten
½ cup raisins
¼ cup chopped pecans
Flour for the work
  surface
Vegetable oil cooking
  spray for greasing
  the pan

1. In a large mixing bowl, stir 1½ cups of the flour and the yeast. In a small saucepan, heat the milk, granulated sugar, butter, and salt over low heat, stirring constantly, until the mixture is lukewarm and the butter has almost melted. Don't let the liquid get too hot—or the yeast won't work.

2. Add the liquid to the flour mixture and beat with an electric mixer set on low speed for 1 minute. Gradually drizzle in the eggs. Beat on low for 30 seconds. Increase the speed to medium; beat about 3 minutes. Stir in the raisins and the chopped pecans. Add enough of the remaining flour so that you have a fairly stiff dough. You can do this part by hand.

3. Lightly flour a work surface. Place the dough on the work surface and knead it with your hands for 6 minutes. When it is smooth and elastic, form it into a ball. Lightly grease the ball with butter. Place the dough in a large bowl, cover with plastic wrap, and let it rise in a warm place for about 2 hours or until double in size.

4. Punch down the dough, re-cover with plastic wrap, and let it rest for 10 minutes.

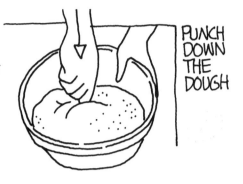

PUNCH DOWN THE DOUGH

For the icing:
1 cup confectioners'
sugar
½ teaspoon vanilla
extract
1½ tablespoons milk
Pecan halves for garnish

PECANS
ICING
3 KINGS CAKE
EPIPHANY

5. Shape the dough into a log and roll it on a lightly floured work surface until it is 18 inches long. Coil and shape it into a 9-inch ring.

6. Grease a Bundt pan with vegetable-oil cooking spray. Place the coil of dough in the pan. Cover and let it rise for about 1 hour or until nearly doubled in size.

7. Preheat the oven to 350°F. Bake the cake for 25 to 30 minutes, until golden brown. Let it cool in the pan for about 10 minutes, then run a spatula around the edges and turn it out onto a wire rack to finish cooling.

8. *Make the icing*: In a small bowl, with an electric mixer set on medium speed, briefly beat the confectioners' sugar, vanilla extract, and 1 tablespoon of the milk. Add the remaining ½ tablespoon of milk and beat until creamy. Drizzle the icing over the cake and garnish the top with pecan halves.

Pepper Nuts

MAKES 9 DOZEN SMALL COOKIES

The German name for these cookies is pfeffernüsse, *and in Sweden they are called* pepparnotter. *The surprise ingredient (you'll never guess it) is pepper! But don't worry; you won't even taste it. Instead, when you bite into one of these crisp little gems you'll taste delicious spices and brown sugar.*

Butter for greasing the baking sheets
¾ cup firmly packed brown sugar
¾ cup granulated sugar
3 eggs
Grated rind of 1 lemon
½ cup finely chopped blanched almonds
2½ cups all-purpose flour plus extra for work surface
1 teaspoon baking powder
1 teaspoon ground cinnamon
½ teaspoon ground cloves
½ teaspoon ground allspice
¼ teaspoon ground black pepper
½ cup confectioners' sugar for rolling the cookies

1. Lightly butter some baking sheets.

2. In a large mixing bowl, with an electric mixer set on medium speed, beat the brown sugar, granulated sugar, and eggs for 2 minutes. Add the lemon rind and the chopped almonds; beat for 1 minute.

3. Sift 2½ cups flour, baking powder, cinnamon, cloves, allspice, and black pepper. Add the flour mixture to the egg mixture; stir with a wooden spoon until a dough is formed.

   BLACK PEPPER (NO KIDDING!)

4. Turn dough out onto a floured work surface and knead with the heel of your hand until it is smooth. Add a bit more flour if needed so the dough isn't sticky. Shape the dough into long rolls, each about 1 inch in diameter. Cut the cookies into ½-inch-thick slices and place them 2 inches apart on the prepared baking sheets. Allow to dry, uncovered, overnight.

5. Preheat the oven to 350°F. Bake the cookies for 15 to 20 minutes, until brown.

6. Remove the cookies from the oven. Place the confectioners' sugar on a shallow plate. Roll the cookies in the sugar while they are still warm. They will last for weeks in a tightly covered container.

Finger-Lickin' Good Blinchiki

You can roll these up and fill them with applesauce, or just spread them with preserves and roll up with your fingers. Either way, they make a delicious dessert.

2 eggs
1 teaspoon sugar
⅛ teaspoon salt
2 cups whole milk
2 cups all-purpose flour
Butter for greasing the pan
Jam for the filling

For the topping:
Confectioners' sugar

1. In a medium bowl, lightly beat the eggs with an electric mixer set on medium speed. Add the sugar and salt and beat for 1 minute. Add the milk gradually, continuing to beat. Add the flour, ¼ cup at a time, beating until thoroughly incorporated after each addition. The batter should be smooth and thin, like heavy cream. If it seems too thick, add a couple more tablespoons of milk.

2. Heat a large heavy frying pan over medium heat. When it is hot, grease it very lightly with butter. In the frying pan, form pancakes that are about 4 inches in diameter. Fry on one side for 1 minute or until golden brown, then turn and fry for a few seconds on the other side.

3. Remove from the pan. Spread the cooked *blinchiki* with jam and roll them up. Place them in a baking pan and continue to make more and fill them with jam. Dust the *blinchiki* liberally with confectioners' sugar and serve.

Russian Walnut Butter Cookies

In Russian these cookies are called "kurabieh." In any language, they are delicious and very elegant.

1 egg yolk
1 cup (2 sticks) unsalted butter, at room temperature
⅓ cup confectioners' sugar
1 teaspoon vanilla extract
½ cup finely chopped walnuts
2¼ cups all-purpose flour
½ teaspoon baking powder

For coating the cookies:
⅓ cup confectioners' sugar

1. Preheat the oven to 350°F. In a small bowl, lightly beat the egg yolk with a fork; set aside.

2. In a large mixing bowl, with an electric mixer set on medium speed, beat the butter for 2 minutes or until light and creamy. Add ⅓ cup of the confectioners' sugar; beat for 1 minute. Beat in the egg yolk and the vanilla. Add the walnuts and beat briefly.

3. Into a medium bowl, sift the flour and the baking powder. Add the flour mixture to the butter mixture in three parts, beating well after each addition.

4. To form the cookies, roll the dough into little balls and place them 1 inch apart on ungreased baking sheets. Bake for 18 to 20 minutes, until golden and firm. Remove from the oven and allow to cool slightly.

5. After about 10 minutes, place the remaining ⅓ cup of confectioners' sugar on a plate. Gently roll the cookies in the sugar.

WALNUT BUTTER COOKIES

Banana Blast Nog

This is so creamy and good that grown-ups may help themselves, too. Besides being festive, it's healthy!

2 ripe bananas
1½ cups milk (whole or lowfat)
½ cup plain or vanilla yogurt
3 tablespoons honey
1 teaspoon vanilla extract
3 ice cubes
Freshly grated nutmeg for garnish

Peel the bananas and cut them into chunks. Place them in a blender. Add the milk, yogurt, honey, vanilla, and ice cubes. Whirl until creamy, about 1 minute. Serve in punch cups with a little nutmeg grated on top.

Valentine's Day

Medieval folk tradition claims that the springtime mating of birds took place on St. Valentine's Day and that this is what developed into the custom of choosing a valentine, or a sweetheart, for the day by holding a random drawing. The randomly chosen "lovers" exchanged messages of affection, and these notes were what ultimately led up to what we know as valentines. For about the last two hundred years, commercial valentines have been for sale in shops.

It's generally believed that Valentine's Day has been celebrated since the Middle Ages, and nearly everyone agrees that it's to honor St. Valentine. The only problem is: There are about eight St. Valentines! So since it would be impossible to figure out which one to pay attention to, let's just figure we'll observe the day with plenty of good things to eat.

When we were little, my parents used to give each of us a little bag of "conversation hearts," which had messages written on them such as "Be Mine" and "You're Sweet." Sometimes, we also received a small clear-plastic heart filled with gold-wrapped chocolate coins. We used to make these chocolate disks last as long as possible by eating very slowly; chocolate was a sweet commodity that didn't appear very often in our house.

On Valentine's Day I like to present each of my children with a chocolate surprise because, after all, chocolate is the ultimate treat on this holiday. You can get your chocolate fix with candies, ice cream, or a sumptuous, tender layer cake swathed in chocolate frosting.

One of the easiest, richest, and most chocolaty candies to make at home are truffles. Real truffles are actually very expensive fungi that grow underground near the roots of trees in some parts of the world. Searched out by trained pigs or even dogs, they're a great treat. Pigs are better for this purpose than dogs, by the way, because they have keener noses.

Chocolate truffles look something like real truffles, but they are sweet and creamy. You could put a dozen into a little box lined with pink or red tissue paper and give them to someone you love.

Another traditional dessert for this day is a cheese and cream dessert called *coeur à la crème*, which is French for "heart with cream." In France, it's a heart-shaped sweet made in a special mold with cream cheese, heavy cream, and eggs. After the dessert is made, it's refrigerated overnight so that the whey, or the liquid, drains out. Then the dessert is unmolded and garnished with strawberries, which, if you really look at them, resemble hearts, too.

If you're taking cupcakes to school, pink is the obvious color for frosting, right? You could also sprinkle the tops with red-colored sugar. In terms of what to drink, Valentine's Day falls smack in the middle of winter, when hot chocolate is the quintessential beverage. Instead of using the powdered mixes, do it from scratch. You'll probably wind up making it on snowy days when you come in from sledding or skating, too.

By the way, a couple of important tips for when you work with chocolate. Never use a wooden spoon to stir chocolate as it melts; the spoon could be holding water from when it was washed hours earlier, and water is chocolate's enemy. Instead of a whisk, use a regular metal spoon. Chocolate can be a little temperamental, so be very careful not to overheat or to overbeat it.

Easy Dark-Chocolate Truffle Balls

MAKES 2 DOZEN

Lush and rich, these are the essence of what a good chocolate candy should be. Rolling them into balls is fun for kids of all ages.

½ pound semisweet
   chocolate
½ cup heavy cream
½ cup confectioners'
   sugar or chopped nuts
   (optional)
Cocoa power for dusting
   your hands

1. Chop the chocolate into very tiny pieces. Place it in a large mixing bowl.

2. In a small saucepan, heat the cream over medium heat. Pour the hot cream over the chocolate all at once. Stir slowly with a dry metal spoon until the mixture is smooth. Cover tightly. Cool to room temperature. Refrigerate for 3 to 4 hours, until thick.

3. Line a baking sheet with parchment paper. Use a melon baller to shape the chocolate into ¾-inch balls and place them on the sheet. Cover loosely with plastic wrap. Refrigerate until firm, 2 to 3 hours.

4. Dust your hands with a bit of cocoa powder and roll the truffles into perfect balls. If you like, roll them in confectioners' sugar or chopped nuts. Store the truffles, covered, in the refrigerator and eat them within 3 weeks, or you may freeze them for up to 2 months.

Chocolate Lover's Hot Cocoa with Vanilla Whipped Cream

SERVES 6

For the hot chocolate:
1/2 cup granulated sugar
1/4 cup unsweetened cocoa powder
Pinch of salt
1/3 cup very hot water
4 cups milk
1 teaspoon vanilla extract

For the topping:
1 cup heavy cream, well chilled
1/4 cup confectioners' sugar
1/2 teaspoon vanilla extract

1. *Make the hot chocolate:* In a large, heavy saucepan, stir the sugar, cocoa powder, and salt. Slowly stir in the hot water.

2. Bring to a boil over medium heat. Boil, stirring constantly, for 2 minutes.

3. Reduce the heat to low. Stir in the milk and heat until very hot but *not* boiling. Remove from the heat and stir in the vanilla.

4. *Make the whipped cream:* With a handheld electric mixer set on high speed, beat the heavy cream. When the cream begins to thicken, add the confectioners' sugar and the vanilla. Keep beating until soft peaks of whipped cream form.

5. Ladle the hot cocoa into mugs or cups. Top each serving with a large puff of whipped cream.

Milk-Chocolate Three-Layer Cake

A tall, festive, light chocolate cake, this is best when served with cold milk or a scoop of slightly softened vanilla ice cream. Or, in keeping with the colors of Valentine's Day, garnish each slice with a few beautiful strawberries.

Vegetable shortening for greasing the pans
2 (1-ounce) squares unsweetened chocolate
2¼ cups sugar (divided)
¾ cup butter (1½ sticks), at room temperature
4 eggs, separated
1 teaspoon vanilla extract
2¼ cups all-purpose flour
1 teaspoon cream of tartar
½ teaspoon baking soda
1 cup milk

1. Preheat the oven to 350°F. Lightly grease three 9-inch layer cake pans. Line the bottoms with waxed paper and grease the waxed paper.

2. In a small glass bowl, heat the chocolate in the microwave oven on High for 30 seconds, until melted; stir. If not melted, heat for another 30 seconds and stir again. Repeat until melted. Keep in mind that chocolate continues to hold its shape even when it is about to melt, so check on this by stirring it! Set the melted chocolate aside to cool.

VALENTINES DAY

A GREAT COMBINATION ♥

CAKE AND A GLASS OF MILK!

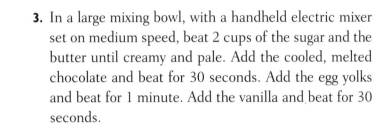

3. In a large mixing bowl, with a handheld electric mixer set on medium speed, beat 2 cups of the sugar and the butter until creamy and pale. Add the cooled, melted chocolate and beat for 30 seconds. Add the egg yolks and beat for 1 minute. Add the vanilla and beat for 30 seconds.

4. Sift the flour, cream of tartar, and baking soda. Add half of this mixture to the batter and beat for 1 minute. Add the milk and beat for 1 minute. Add the remaining flour mixture and beat for 1 minute.

5. Wash the beaters. In another mixing bowl, beat the egg whites on high speed until they are frothy. Add the remaining ¼ cup sugar to the whites and beat again for a minute or two, until stiff peaks form when you lift up the beater. Gently fold the beaten egg whites into the batter. Use a spatula, not the electric mixer, for this.

6. Spoon and scrape the batter into the prepared pans. Bake for 25 to 30 minutes, until the tops are set and the middle of the layer springs back when you press it with your finger. Allow the layers to cool in the pans for 10 minutes. Run a knife around the edge of each pan. Gently invert each cake layer onto a wire rack to cool. Carefully peel off the waxed paper. Allow the cake to cool completely before frosting with Chocolate Cream Cheese Frosting.

SPREAD ICING

Chocolate Cream Cheese Frosting

4 (1-ounce) squares semisweet chocolate

6 ounces cream cheese, at room temperature

4 tablespoons whole milk

4 cups sifted confectioners' sugar

2 teaspoons vanilla extract

1. In a small glass bowl, heat the squares of chocolate in the microwave oven on high for 60 seconds, until melted; stir. If not melted, heat for another 20 seconds and stir again. Keep in mind that chocolate continues to hold its shape even when it's on the verge of melting, so check on this by stirring it! Set the chocolate aside to cool.

2. In a large mixing bowl, with an electric mixer set on high speed, beat the cooled chocolate, cream cheese, and milk. Sift in the sugar and beat well. Beat in the vanilla extract. Beat on high until smooth and creamy. Use immediately or refrigerate for up to 3 days.

Cupid's Cupcakes with Pink Frosting

You can easily double this recipe if you need enough cupcakes for your whole class. Tint the icing with a couple of drops of red food coloring to get the color of icing you like. For an extra-festive touch, decorate the cupcake tops with conversation hearts or with a halved maraschino cherry.

1¼ cups all-purpose
   flour
1½ teaspoons baking
   powder
Pinch of salt
6 tablespoons (¾ stick)
   butter, at room
   temperature
⅔ cup sugar
3 egg yolks
¾ teaspoon vanilla
   extract
½ cup milk

1. Preheat the oven to 350°F. Line 12 muffin cups with paper liners.

2. Into a large mixing bowl, sift the flour, baking powder, and salt; set aside.

3. In a medium mixing bowl, beat the butter with an electric mixer set on high speed for 2 minutes. Gradually beat in the sugar and beat for 1 minute. Add the egg yolks, 1 at a time, and beat on medium speed just until blended. Beat in the vanilla.

4. Beat in ½ the flour mixture on low speed and continue to beat just until blended. Add the milk and beat until blended. Add the remaining flour mixture and beat just until blended. Spoon the batter into the paper liners.

5. Bake the cupcakes for about 20 minutes or until the tops spring back when pressed with a fingertip. Cool completely on a wire rack before frosting with Pink Frosting.

Pink Frosting

This recipe makes enough frosting so that you can lavishly frost each cupcake and still have extra for another cake.

½ cup (1 stick) butter, at room temperature
1 (8-ounce) package cream cheese, at room temperature
1 teaspoon vanilla extract
⅛ teaspoon salt
1½ cups confectioners' sugar
Few drops of red food coloring

1. In a large mixing bowl, beat the butter and cream cheese with an electric mixer on high speed for about 2 minutes, until creamy. Beat in the vanilla and the salt.

2. Add the confectioners' sugar and beat on low speed until well blended. Beat in the food coloring. Refrigerate for 10 minutes before spreading on cupcakes.

PINK ICING FOR VALENTINE'S DAY

HUGS

LOVE KISS

Pretty in Pink
Fresh Strawberry Cheesecake

This is an easy, Americanized version of the French coeur à la crème. *Use a heart-shaped pan or a regular springform pan.*

Butter for greasing the pan
¼ cup (½ stick) butter, melted and cooled
1 cup graham cracker crumbs
¼ cup granulated sugar
2 (8-ounce) packages cream cheese, at room temperature
1 (14-ounce) can sweetened condensed milk
3 eggs, lightly beaten
¼ teaspoon salt
¼ cup lemon juice
1 pint fresh strawberries, washed, hulled, and halved
½ cup confectioners' sugar

1. Preheat the oven to 350°F. Lightly butter a 9-inch heart-shaped pan or a springform pan.

2. *Make the crust:* In a small mixing bowl, combine the butter, graham cracker crumbs, and granulated sugar. Pat firmly onto the bottom of the buttered pan.

3. *Make the filling:* In a large mixing bowl, with an electric mixer set on medium speed, beat the cream cheese for 2 minutes, until fluffy. Beat in the sweetened condensed milk, eggs, and salt. Beat in the lemon juice. Pour and scrape the batter into the pan.

4. Bake for 50 to 55 minutes or until the cake springs back when touched. Remove from the oven and allow to cool. Remove the springform part of the pan. Wrap the cake with plastic wrap. Chill for several hours or overnight. Decorate the top with halved strawberries and sprinkle with confectioners' sugar.

French Chocolate

Pôts de Crème

In French, the name of this luscious custard means "pots of cream," and it is certainly creamy. Traditionally, it's baked and served in teensy, pot-shaped cups, but you can make it in regular ovenproof custard cups. Although the classic pôt de crème is flavored with vanilla, this chocolate variation is great for Valentine's Day.

⅔ cup semisweet
  chocolate chips
1 cup half-and-half
2 eggs
4 tablespoons sugar
Pinch of salt
Whipped cream for
  garnish (optional)

1. Preheat the oven to 350°F. In a medium glass mixing bowl, combine the chocolate chips and half-and-half. Heat for 1–3 minutes in the microwave oven on high, stirring several times. When the chocolate has melted and the mixture is creamy-smooth, stir and set aside to cool.

2. In a medium mixing bowl, beat the eggs with a wire whisk. Add the sugar and the salt and beat until well combined. Gradually stir the egg mixture into the chocolate mixture. Pour into 4 to 6 ungreased ovenproof *pôt-de-crème* cups or custard cups.

3. Place the cups in a baking pan and set the pan on the middle oven rack. Pour enough boiling water into the pan to reach within a half inch of the tops of the cups. Bake for 20 minutes. Remove the baking pan from the oven and remove the custard cups from the pan. Cool on a rack. Cover and refrigerate for at least 4 hours. Garnish with a dollop of whipped cream, if desired.

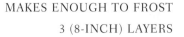

Rich Chocolate Butter Icing

3 ounces baking
chocolate
6 tablespoons whole
milk
3 cups confectioners'
sugar
6 tablespoons (¾ stick)
butter, at room
temperature
Pinch of salt
1 tablespoon vanilla
extract

1. In the top of a double boiler, melt the chocolate over hot but not boiling water.

2. In a medium heavy saucepan, bring the milk to a boil. Remove from the heat and add the confectioners' sugar all at once. With an electric mixer set on medium speed, beat until smooth. Add the melted chocolate. Cool until the mixture is lukewarm.

3. In a large bowl, with the electric mixer set on medium speed, beat the butter for 2 minutes or until creamy. Beat in the salt, vanilla, and cooled chocolate mixture. Spread on cake immediately.

Fruity Chocolate Fondue

SERVES 6 TO 8

Fondue is a fun food for a party. It's like a sauce, and you use special long-handled forks to spear chunks of fruit that you then dip into the fondue. The pot sits over a little flame, so it stays hot. You need a fondue pot for this recipe.

For the fondue:
1 (12-ounce) bag
  semisweet chocolate
  morsels
½ cup sugar
1 teaspoon vanilla
  extract
½ cup light cream

For the fruit:
2 bananas, cut into
  1½-inch-thick chunks
1 pint strawberries,
  stemmed and washed
1 cup pineapple chunks

1. Place the chocolate morsels in the fondue pot. Add the sugar, vanilla, and light cream. Place the fondue pot over direct low heat. Stir until the chocolate has melted and the mixture is smooth. Keep the flame very low so the mixture is just melted and the texture is smooth.

2. Arrange the fruit on a platter. Spear the pieces of fruit with long-handled fondue forks or wooden skewers. Dip into the hot chocolate mixture.

Note: If you don't have a fondue pot, use a double boiler, melting the chocolate, sugar, vanilla, and light cream over simmering water.

CHOCOLATE FONDUE

Valentine's Day **49**

Hot Chocolate Sauce

SERVES 4–8

My mother made this sauce for us as a special treat. It's excellent over strawberry ice cream for Valentine's Day.

¼ cup (½ stick) unsalted butter
1½ squares unsweetened chocolate, finely shaved
¾ cup unsweetened cocoa powder
¾ cup sugar
¼ cup heavy cream
⅛ teaspoon salt
1 teaspoon vanilla extract

1. In the top of a double boiler over simmering water, heat the butter and chocolate until they melt. Stir until smooth.

2. Stir in the cocoa, sugar, cream, and salt. Bring to a simmer but do *not* boil. The sauce should be thick. Remove from the heat, stir in the vanilla, and serve warm.

STRAWBERRY ICE CREAM

Chinese New Year

The focus is on a different animal each year during the Chinese New Year, an important and very festive holiday that's observed according to the lunar calendar. There are a dozen animals in all, one for each year of a twelve-year cycle. They include the Rat, the Ox, the Tiger, the Rabbit, the Dragon, the Snake, the Horse, the Sheep, the Monkey, the Rooster, the Dog, and the Pig.

The Chinese believe that you have certain characteristics depending on which year you were born. This zodiac concept is kind of like our monthly horoscope. Those born in the year of the Dragon are said to be optimistic, brave, and ambitious. People born in the year of the Pig are believed to be peaceful and alert, and intelligent but shy.

Chinese people believe that there also are five phases (fire, water, earth, wood, and metal). Together the five phases and the twelve "zodiac" beasts create a cycle that spans sixty years. For instance, there's a twelve-year cycle during the fire phase, another twelve-year cycle during the earth phase, and another during the water phase.

The Chinese New Year begins on the first day of the first month of the lunar calendar, so it falls somewhere between late January and mid-February. Chinese people begin to get ready for New Year's Day a month in advance. They clean their houses, sweeping out any bad luck from the previous year, and paste up colorful decorations. Because red is considered lucky, the decorations are red, and sometimes people paint their front doors red, too. Plants such as orange and lemon trees may be used to decorate the house.

Inside the Chinese kitchen, which is the center of the home, lives the kitchen god. The family sends him to heaven at New Year so that he can report on the family's activities to the highest god in heaven, the Jade Emperor.

And just how does the kitchen god get sent to heaven, you might wonder? First his lips are smeared with honey so that he will report only good things to the Jade Emperor, then his picture is burned. Then the next day, which is New Year's Day, the kitchen god returns from heaven, and Chinese families hang a new picture of him in the kitchen.

On New Year's Eve, the whole family eats dinner together. They invite their ancestors to the meal, too, and honor these deceased relatives by making sacrifices of food and incense. While this custom might sound morbid, it's actually an occasion for a joyous family reunion.

Families stay up the whole night to make sure no bad luck comes to their house. They have big celebrations, eat dumplings together, and wish one another Happy New Year. Fireworks are set off because it is believed that they can drive away the bad luck and evil spirits of the previous year and attract prosperity for the year to come.

On New Year's Day, people stay home for a quiet day. Children are very respectful of their parents and the older members of their family. Everyone tries not to say or do anything bad, because they believe that this will ensure that good things will happen in the coming year.

During the next few days, everyone visits relatives and friends. Adults give children red envelopes filled with lucky money. People watch lion dances, which are believed to bring good luck to all. Grown-ups give each other gifts like wine, fruit, cakes, candies, and flowers. And whenever friends visit, it's traditional to serve "lucky" foods like dates, peanuts, and lotus seeds.

Food is a central part of Chinese New Year, so the kitchen is typically the busiest place in the house. Chinese people don't eat as many sweets as Westerners do, and, in fact, at an ordinary Chinese dinner there's no dessert at all. But Chinese people love sweets at big banquets. And luckily, Chinese New Year is a time for eating a big banquet. An exception is made to the "no dessert" rule, and families enjoy special sweets during this holiday. To make the desserts in this chapter, you will need to shop at an Asian grocery store or in the ethnic food aisle of the supermarket.

Rice Cake

This recipe comes from Zhao "Sunny" Zeng, an instructor at the China Institute in New York City, who notes that rice cake is supposed to be sticky.

Oil for greasing the pan
2 cups rice flour
I cup glutinous rice flour
I¼ cups water (or maybe a little more or less)
½ cup sugar
Cooked red beans or dried red dates (optional)
4 teaspoons sugar for sprinkling on the rice cake

1. Lightly grease a small baking pan. Place a metal steamer in a large pot of water. Add enough water to the pan to just reach the steamer and place the pot over high heat.

2. In a large bowl, combine the rice flour, glutinous rice flour, water, sugar and cooked red beans or dried red dates. The mixture should have the consistency of a cake batter. If it is very thick, add a bit more water. If it is too runny, add a bit more rice flour.

3. Spoon the batter into the prepared pan. Steam the cake for about 8 minutes or until firm. Sprinkle with sugar, cut into squares, and serve.

Eight-Treasure Sweet Rice

SERVES 4–6

This is another traditional sweet from Zhao "Sunny" Zeng at the China Institute. Glutinous rice is a round, small-grained rice that gets sticky when it is cooked. This is sweet and sticky, which is good, explains Sunny. She says that when your family eats this cake, it means that you're sweet and that you all will stick together. Follow the cooking directions on a package of glutinous rice.

2 cups cooked glutinous rice
2 to 3 tablespoons vegetable oil
3 tablespoons sugar
½ cup red bean paste
Cooked red beans, red dates, raisins or other kinds of dried fruit
Lotus seeds for decoration

1. In a medium bowl, mix the cooked rice, the oil, and sugar.

2. Place a steamer in a large pot. Fill the pot with enough water to reach the steamer and bring to a boil over high heat.

3. In a greased, heatproof bowl, layer half the rice mixture, then the red bean paste, and finish with the remaining rice mixture.

4. Steam the cake for 5 minutes. Invert the steamed cake onto a plate. Decorate the cake with the cooked red beans, red dates, raisins or other dried fruits, and lotus seeds.

Note: If you only have six types of decorations, then this dessert becomes Six-Treasure Sweet Rice.

Almond Cookies

Crunchy and good on their own or with a fruit salad.

Butter for greasing the baking sheets
¾ cup sugar
½ cup (1 stick) unsalted butter, at room temperature
2 eggs
1¼ cups all-purpose flour
½ teaspoon baking soda
½ teaspoon salt
1 cup finely chopped almonds
¾ teaspoon almond extract
36 whole almonds

1. Preheat the oven to 350°F. Lightly butter 2 baking sheets.

2. In a medium mixing bowl, with an electric mixer set on medium speed, beat the sugar and ½ cup butter for 5 minutes. Add 1 of the eggs and beat until smooth.

3. Into a separate mixing bowl, sift the flour, baking soda, and salt. Beat into the butter mixture in 3 additions. Beat until smooth. Add the chopped almonds and the almond extract; mix until smooth.

4. Drop tablespoons of the batter onto the prepared baking sheets about 1 inch apart. Dip your thumb in some flour and make an indentation in the center of each cookie.

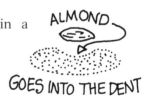

MAKE A DENT WITH YOUR THUMB

5. Beat the remaining egg in a small bowl. Brush each cookie with beaten egg and place an almond in each indentation.

ALMOND GOES INTO THE DENT

6. Bake the cookies for 10 minutes or until they are golden brown and slightly puffed. Remove from the oven, cool 2 minutes, and then use a spatula to transfer them to a rack. Cool completely.

Candied Walnuts

These make a very delicious snack, but parents should definitely do the cooking here, as deep frying is a no-no for kids. Young cooks can help by tossing the drained walnuts with the sugar.

1 pound (about 4 cups) shelled walnuts
1½ cups sugar
4 cups vegetable oil

1. In a large pot of boiling water, simmer the walnuts for 5 minutes; drain them well. Toss them with the sugar. Shake the walnuts to remove excess sugar. Spread them out on a baking sheet to dry.

2. In a wok, heat the oil over high heat until hot but not smoking. Fry the walnuts in several batches for 1 minute, until they are golden. Drain them on a baking sheet lined with paper towels.

Poached Tangerines

SERVES 6

Tangerines are considered a fruit of good fortune by Chinese families.

5½ cups water
6 tangerines
1½ cups sugar
3 cinnamon sticks
4 small slices fresh
   ginger
2 teaspoons rice vinegar

1. In a heavy saucepan, bring the water to a simmer. Meanwhile, peel the tangerines and discard the strings.

2. When the water simmers, add the sugar, cinnamon, and ginger. Cook, stirring occasionally, for 30 minutes. Carefully add the tangerines to the water and simmer for 10 minutes.

3. Remove the tangerines from the simmering water and place them in a bowl. Boil the water for about 20 more minutes, until it is reduced to 2 cups. Stir in the rice vinegar. Strain the syrup over the tangerines and cover tightly with plastic wrap. Refrigerate overnight.

VERY CAREFULLY ADD PEELED TANGERINES TO HOT LIQUID

POACHED TANGERINES

PEEL

Orange Slices with Brown Sugar

SERVES 4

You can make this a few hours ahead and refrigerate until serving time.

4 navel oranges
4 tablespoons brown
  sugar
¾ teaspoon ground
  cinnamon

1. Peel the oranges; cut them into slices. Arrange the slices on a platter.

2. Stir together the brown sugar and cinnamon. Sprinkle this mixture over the oranges. Allow the oranges to sit at room temperature for 10 minutes before serving.

Chinese Fruit Salad

SERVES 6

This refreshing salad has some exotic fruits in it. Loquats, also known as Japanese plums, are pear-shaped but more the color of an apricot and taste something like cherries. Since they are very fragile, they usually aren't shipped great distances, so we mostly get them canned. Litchis are juicy and have a delicate flavor. You can sometimes buy them fresh, but their season is very short. Canned litchis and loquats work very well in this salad.

½ **cantaloupe**
2 **cups strawberries**
3 **tablespoons sugar**
I **can (about 20 ounces) litchis in syrup**
I **can (about 15 ounces) loquats in syrup**
I **cup apple juice**

1. Scoop out balls of melon using a melon baller. You'll need about 2 cups. Place the cantaloupe balls in a pretty serving bowl.

2. Wash and dry the strawberries. Hull the berries and cut the large ones in half. Add them to the cantaloupe and toss with the sugar.

3. Drain the cans of litchis and loquats. Save about ⅓ cup of the juice from each can. Add the litchis and the loquats to the cantaloupe balls and strawberries. Pour the reserved juice over the fruit.

4. Pour on the apple juice. Gently stir to mix up the fruits. Cover and refrigerate until it's time for dessert.

St. Patrick's Day

There's one day out of each year when everyone is Irish, wearing bright green is definitely considered cool, and bakeries try to outdo one other selling green bagels, cupcakes, breads, and cookies. It's March 17, St. Patrick's Day, an occasion to honor a very special saint.

In Ireland, where St. Patrick lived, the day is a bank holiday, and many restaurants and stores are closed. Here in the United States, many cities have enormous parades, with floats, Irish dancing, and politicians galore.

Years ago, St. Patrick's Day was always the occasion of my parents' annual party. There was plenty of lively conversation, lots to drink, and good-natured joking about which country was superior: Scotland or Ireland. My father is Scottish and my mother was mostly Irish, and their friends were either one, the other, or both.

Our house, after being scrubbed and shined in honor of the saint, was decorated with green balloons. There also were one or two orange ones (representing Scotland). Before we went to bed, my parents' dear friend Herb Connolly would make a great show of chasing us kids around as he tried to pop the orange balloons we'd hold out of his reach. Giggling and silly, we'd race around the house as he feigned a villainous look and pretended that he couldn't catch up with us. The younger children were then tucked into bed, but we older ones were permitted to stay up and lay out the food: hot and cold salads and casseroles, overstuffed sandwiches from the local delicatessen, green gelatin molds and fruit salads.

My mother's friends brought enough casseroles, salads, and stews to nourish our entire town for a month, but what I remember most were the desserts. A moist, crumbly sour cream coffee cake, fudgy brownies, and my father's specialty, peanut cakes, a delicious confection that he had invented himself and was very proud of. Peanut cakes are small slices of white cake that are immersed in white icing and then rolled in chopped peanuts. Biting into one of these cakes is kind of like tasting a peanut butter sandwich, vanilla cupcake, and peanut butter cup all at the same time. For me, they will always be synonymous with St. Patrick's Day.

We all watched my father prepare his specialty early on the day of the party, arranging them on waxed paper in a single layer to dry. The first time I tried making them, the cakes fell apart when I tried to ice them. So my father shared his secret: freeze the little oblongs for a while before you ice them, and they'll stay firm enough to withstand the handling. And keep the icing thin enough so the cake doesn't break apart.

I thought my parents' parties would go forever, but after the sudden death of Herb Connolly from a stroke, the parties seemed more subdued and smaller. As my parents' friends grew older, my mother decided to put out the food before midnight so that everyone could get home to bed earlier. Eventually the parties did grow more subdued, and smaller, too, until they finally stopped altogether. It was one of those childhood traditions that came to an end so gradually that I didn't miss it at first. Of course, by then I had a baby daughter of my own and was working full time.

My husband and I never threw big St. Patrick's Day parties, but as our family has grown, we always mark the occasion with a special meal. For dessert, there are always green frosted shamrock cookies— and peanut cakes, too, for old time's sake.

Peanut Lover's Peanut Cakes

You could use a boxed mix for this recipe, but a cake made from scratch takes just minutes longer and tastes so much better. My father likes to make a cake that uses whites only (no yolks).

Vegetable shortening
and flour for coating
the baking pan
1¾ cups cake flour
2 teaspoons baking
powder
¼ teaspoon salt
⅔ cup butter, at room
temperature
1 cup sugar
3 egg whites
1 teaspoon vanilla
extract
½ cup cold water
1 recipe White Icing (see
below)
2 cups dry-roasted
peanuts

1. Preheat the oven to 350°F. Lightly grease and flour two 9-inch square baking pans.

2. Into a medium mixing bowl, sift the flour, baking powder, and salt.

3. In a large mixing bowl, with an electric mixer on medium speed, beat the butter until very soft. Add the sugar gradually and beat thoroughly, about 2 minutes. Add 1 egg white and beat for a minute. Add another egg white and beat for 1 minute. Add the last egg white and beat again for 1 minute. Add the vanilla extract and the water and beat 1 minute. Add the flour mixture and beat for 2 minutes, until the batter is smooth.

4. Pour and scrape the batter into the prepared pans. Bake 15 minutes or until a toothpick inserted into the center of the cake comes out clean. Remove from the oven and cool the cakes in the pans for 15 minutes.

5. When the cakes are cool, cut them into rectangles approximately 3 inches by 1 inch. Place the little cakes in a single layer on a baking sheet. Cover and freeze for at least 2 hours.

6. Make Luscious White Icing and have it ready in a large mixing bowl. You want it to be fairly runny. Chop the peanuts in a food processor. Be sure to process them only until coarsely chopped—you don't want them to turn into peanut butter! Place chopped peanuts on a plate.

PEANUT CAKE

1"x3"   3"x1"

INTO ICING   INTO PEANUTS   DRY ON WAXED PAPER

7. Roll each piece of cake in the icing until completely coated and then immediately roll it in the chopped nuts. Place each cake on waxed paper. Allow the cakes to dry completely. Store the cakes with a sheet of waxed paper between the layers in a tin with a tight-fitting lid.

Luscious White Icing

MAKES ENOUGH TO ICE 4–5
DOZEN PEANUT CAKES

When I have leftover icing, my kids drizzle it onto graham cracker squares and sandwich them together for an afterschool snack. You can also use this to ice home-made oatmeal cookies.

3 cups confectioners' sugar
⅓ cup (or slightly more) whole milk

Into a large mixing bowl, sift the confectioners' sugar. Add the milk and beat with an electric mixer set on medium speed until smooth. Be sure to beat thoroughly until the icing is lump free. It should be runny enough so that you can easily roll the cakes in it. If not, beat in another tablespoon of milk.

Mom's Fudgiest Ever Brownies

MAKES 2 DOZEN

These rich, fudgy squares are wonderful with a glass of milk. If you like nuts in your brownies, add a cup of chopped walnuts or pecans after the vanilla extract.

Cooking spray for the pan
4 (1-ounce) squares unsweetened baking chocolate
1 cup (2 sticks) unsalted butter, cut into quarters
2 cups sugar
4 eggs
1½ cups all-purpose flour
1½ teaspoons baking powder
1 teaspoon salt
1 teaspoon vanilla extract

1. Preheat the oven to 350°F. Lightly spray a 9 by 13-inch baking pan with cooking spray.

2. In a large mixing bowl, place the chocolate and the butter. Heat in the microwave oven on Medium until melted, stirring every 30 seconds. Set aside to cool.

3. When the chocolate has thoroughly cooled, with an electric mixer set on medium speed, beat in the sugar. Beat in the eggs, one at a time.

4. Into a medium bowl, sift together the flour, baking powder, and salt. Sift the flour mixture into the chocolate mixture. Beat 1 minute on medium speed. Add the vanilla and beat for 30 seconds or until the batter is thoroughly mixed.

5. Spoon and scrape the batter into the prepared pan. Bake for 20 to 25 minutes, until the brownies are firm but still slightly sticky in the center. These are easy to overbake, so watch them carefully. Cut into squares when cool. Ice with Chocolate Glaze. (Heat 1 cup chocolate chips with 4 tablespoons of butter, stirring frequently. Add 1 teaspoon vanilla extract and stir.)

Emerald Isle Irish Soda Bread

It's a fine day to eat Irish soda bread, a slightly sweet round loaf that can contain raisins and caraway seeds (or not, if you don't like them). This is an easy-to-make dessert that's leavened with baking soda rather than yeast. Spread with sweet butter and enjoy with a cup of decaffeinated tea or milk.

Flour for the work surface

2 cups white flour

2 teaspoons baking powder

2 teaspoons baking soda

3/4 teaspoon salt

4 tablespoons granulated sugar

3 tablespoons unsalted butter, at room temperature

1 cup buttermilk

1/2 cup raisins

3 tablespoons confectioners' sugar for topping

1. Preheat the oven to 375°F. Lightly flour work surface.

2. Into a large mixing bowl, sift the flour, baking powder, baking soda, salt, and sugar. Use 2 table knives or your fingers to cut in the butter until the mixture resembles coarse peas. Stir in the buttermilk with a large wooden spoon. Add the raisins and mix just until no traces of flour are visible.

3. Form the dough into a ball and place it on a floured work surface. Knead it lightly for a minute with the heel of your hand. Gather it into a ball again and pat it into the shape of a round loaf. Place the loaf on an ungreased baking sheet.

4. With a sharp knife, make a large cross in the middle of the loaf. Sprinkle the top with the confectioners' sugar. Bake on the middle rack of the oven for 35 to 40 minutes. Remove when the bread is brown on top and has a nice golden crust on the bottom. Serve warm with butter and jam.

Breakfast Raisin Oatmeal Cookies

Even if you hate oatmeal, you'll love these cookies. They're especially good for breakfast when you're rushing out the door.

Cooking spray for the
  baking sheets
1 cup sugar
½ cup (1 stick) unsalted
  butter, at room
  temperature
2 eggs
1½ teaspoons vanilla
  extract
1½ cups uncooked
  oatmeal (the quick-
  cooking kind, not the
  instant)
1½ cups all-purpose flour
½ teaspoon baking
  powder
½ teaspoon baking soda
½ teaspoon salt
1¼ teaspoons ground
  cinnamon
¼ cup milk
1 cup raisins

1. Preheat the oven to 350°F. Lightly spray 2 baking sheets with cooking spray.

2. In a large mixing bowl, with an electric mixer set on medium speed, beat the sugar and butter until fluffy, about 2 minutes. Add the eggs and beat 1 minute. Add the vanilla and beat 1 minute. Stir in the oatmeal with a big spoon.

3. Into a medium bowl, sift together the flour, baking powder, baking soda, salt, and cinnamon. Add half of this flour mixture to the butter mixture and stir. Beat in the milk with the electric mixer. Add the remaining flour mixture and beat until well incorporated, about 1 minute. Stir in the raisins.

4. Drop the dough by heaping teaspoonfuls 2 inches apart onto the prepared baking sheets. Bake the cookies for 10 to 12 minutes, until the edges are brown. Remove from the oven. With a spatula, transfer the cookies to a rack to finish cooling.

St. Paddy's Bread and Butter Pudding

This pudding has been a traditional favorite for cooks looking for a way to use up leftover bread. But these days, it's a stylish dessert in high-end Irish restaurants, too. In Ireland, grown-ups eat it with whiskey sauce, but it tastes much better topped with lightly sweetened whipped cream.

Butter for greasing the baking pan
¼ cup raisins
½ cup hot water
3 eggs
4 tablespoons (½ stick) unsalted butter, at room temperature
10 slices white bread
1 cup milk
1 cup heavy cream
2½ teaspoons vanilla extract
¾ cup superfine sugar
Pinch of nutmeg
½ teaspoon ground cinnamon

For the topping:
1 cup heavy whipping cream
4 tablespoons confectioners' sugar

1. Preheat the oven to 350°F. Lightly butter an 8-inch round baking dish.

2. In a small bowl, combine raisins and water. Allow to soak for 10 minutes. In another small bowl, beat the eggs with a whisk.

3. Butter the bread. Remove the crusts and cut each slice in half diagonally. Arrange half the slices, buttered side up, in the baking dish. Drain the raisins and discard the water. Sprinkle the raisins over the bread.

4. In a heavy saucepan, combine the milk, cream, vanilla, superfine sugar, nutmeg, and cinnamon. Cook over medium heat for 6 minutes or until the mixture just begins to boil. Remove from the heat and stir in the eggs. Arrange the remaining bread slices over the raisins. Pour the egg custard over the top and allow to stand for 10 minutes. Cover with foil.

5. Place the baking dish inside a large baking pan and add enough hot water to the large pan to reach halfway up the sides of the baking dish. Bake for 50

minutes, until the custard is firm. Cool for 5 minutes in the baking pan before removing. Finish cooling on the counter.

6. *Make the topping:* Whip the cream with an electric mixer set on high speed. When soft peaks form, add the confectioners' sugar and beat until the peaks are stiff. Top each serving of bread pudding with whipped cream.

Irish ☆ Oatmeal-Apple Crumble

SERVES 6–8

Use Irish oatmeal if you can, to make this dish even more authentic. The best kind I have found is McCann's Irish Oatmeal.

Butter for greasing the
  baking pan
6 Granny Smith apples
1 cup sugar
1 cup all-purpose flour
1 cup (2 sticks) butter,
  at room temperature,
  cut into small pieces
4 tablespoons quick-
  cooking oats
½ teaspoon ground
  ginger
1 teaspoon ground
  cinnamon

1. Preheat the oven to 375°F. Lightly butter an 8-inch square baking dish.

2. Peel and core the apples. Slice each apple into 6 wedges. Arrange the wedges in the prepared baking dish, slightly overlapping.

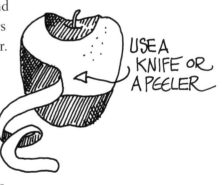

PEELER

USE A KNIFE OR A PEELER

3. In a medium mixing bowl, combine the sugar and flour. Use your fingers to work in the butter. When it has the consistency of large crumbs, add the oatmeal, ginger, and cinnamon. Spread the topping evenly over the apples.

4. Bake, uncovered, for 40 minutes, until the apples are soft and the topping is golden brown. Serve warm, accompanied by vanilla ice cream, if desired.

GREAT WITH VANILLA ICECREAM

Erin Go Bragh Sticky Super-Easy Cinnamon Rolls

These taste a bit like the braided, yeast-raised coffee cake my mother made for St. Patrick's Day, but they're easier to make because they're leavened with baking powder, not yeast. When my daughter Molly used to make these for special company, she'd frost the rolls and decorate them with halved maraschino cherries.

Cooking spray for greasing the muffin tins
4 cups sifted all-purpose flour plus extra for work surface
4 teaspoons baking powder
2 teaspoons salt
¾ cup vegetable shortening
1⅓ cups milk
½ cup (1 stick) butter, at room temperature
½ cup brown sugar
1 teaspoon ground cinnamon
Vanilla Icing (see page 235), optional
Maraschino cherry halves (optional)

1. Preheat the oven to 425°F. Spray 24 muffin cups with cooking spray.

2. Into a large bowl, sift the flour, baking powder, and salt. Add the shortening and rub it in with your hands until the mixture has the consistency of coarse crumbs. Add the milk slowly and stir with a large wooden spoon until a soft dough forms.

3. Turn the dough out onto a lightly floured work surface and knead several times. Using a rolling pin, roll out the dough to a ¼-inch thickness. Spread with the softened butter and then sprinkle with brown sugar and cinnamon.

4. Roll up the dough jelly-roll style as tightly as possible. Cut the roll crosswise into 24 slices. Place 1 slice in each muffin cup. Bake for 15 minutes or until golden brown. Cool the rolls in the tins for 5 minutes. Remove to a rack and allow to finish cooling.

ROLL UP JELLY-ROLL STYLE AND SLICE

5. If you like, spread with Vanilla Icing and decorate with maraschino cherry halves.

Shimmery Shamrock Butter Cookies

A shamrock cookie cutter makes these cookies a breeze. If you prefer not to frost them, sprinkle with green-colored sugar before baking.

¹/₃ cup butter or margarine, at room temperature

¹/₃ cup vegetable shortening

³/₄ cup sugar

1 teaspoon baking powder

Pinch of salt

1 egg

1 teaspoon vanilla extract

2 cups all-purpose flour plus extra for the work surface

St. Patrick's Green Cookie Icing (see following recipe)

1. In a large mixing bowl, with an electric mixer set on medium speed, beat the butter and shortening for 2 minutes. Add the sugar, baking powder, and salt and beat for 2 minutes. Beat in the egg and vanilla. Beat in 1 cup of the flour. Stir in the remaining flour by hand. Cover the dough and refrigerate for 1 hour.

2. Preheat the oven to 325°F. Divide the dough in half. With a rolling pin, roll out one-half on a lightly floured work surface to about a ¹/₈-inch thickness. Cut out with shamrock cookie cutters. (Place on ungreased cookie sheets about 1 inch apart. Repeat with the remaining dough.

3. Bake for about 7 to 8 minutes, until edges are firm and bottoms are lightly browned. Remove from the oven and cool on a wire rack. When cool, frost with St. Patrick's Green Cookie Icing.

SPRINKLE GREEN-COLORED SUGAR (BEFORE BAKING)

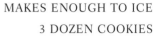

St. Patrick's Green Cookie Icing

91 cup confectioners' sugar
2 teaspoons milk
2 teaspoons light corn syrup (or more if needed)
¼ teaspoon almond extract
5 drops green food coloring

In a small mixing bowl, with an electric mixer set on medium speed, beat the sugar and milk until blended. Add the remaining ingredients and beat until smooth. If the icing is too thick to spread, add 1 to 2 teaspoons more corn syrup.

St. Joseph's Day

Just two days after a feast day in honor of St. Patrick, along comes one on March 19 that honors Saint Joseph, the father of Jesus, who is especially beloved by generations of Italians and Italian Americans. Often pictured as an old, bearded man, St. Joseph is held in high regard for his role as a loving husband and devoted father. In Italy, March 19 is like Father's Day.

The holiday honoring this saint actually began in Sicily during the Middle Ages. During a severe drought, desperate people asked Joseph, their patron, to intervene. If the rain fell, they promised, they would cook a huge feast in his honor. When their prayers were answered with plenty of rainfall, large banquet tables were set up and poor people invited to come and eat their fill.

To this day, generosity is a major theme of this occasion. In cities with a large Italian population, celebrants have plays and processions. They eat plenty of sweets, including rich Italian pastries filled with whipped cream and fruit. It is a day for sharing with the poor and the needy, and in Italian villages, particularly in Sicily, those who can afford to, contribute to a table spread out in the public square. These are offerings for the favors that were received by praying to this saint, whose name in Italian is Giuseppe.

When everyone—beggars, orphans, and widows included—is seated at the table, the priest blesses the food, and everyone shouts, *"Viva tavola di San Giuseppe!"* Then the celebrants eat a filling and hearty meal with a vegetarian soup and various dishes made with dried beans. But thank goodness, there also are many sweets. And there's a special bread for this day that may be shaped like a scepter or a beard.

St. Joseph Doughnuts

(Sfinge de San Giuseppe)

Actually more like a fritter, these tender doughnuts are gently spiced with nutmeg and are best eaten warm on the same day you make them. If you like, reheat them the next day in the microwave oven on medium heat, for about thirty seconds per two doughnuts. Although these are traditionally fried, this version is baked instead.

Vegetable oil for
  greasing the baking
  sheets
1 pound ricotta cheese
½ cup granulated sugar
1 teaspoon vanilla
  extract
½ teaspoon ground
  nutmeg
6 eggs, lightly beaten
  with a fork
2 cups self-rising flour
1 cup confectioners'
  sugar or cinnamon-
  sugar for sprinkling on
  doughnuts

1. Preheat the oven to 400°F. Lightly grease 2 baking sheets.

2. In a large bowl, combine the ricotta, granulated sugar, vanilla, nutmeg, and eggs. Beat well with an electric mixer set on medium speed.

3. Sift the flour into the bowl and beat until smooth. Drop large spoonfuls of the batter 2 inches apart onto the prepared baking sheet.

4. Bake for about 15 minutes or until golden brown. Remove from the oven and use a spatula to transfer them to a rack.

5. Measure the confectioners' sugar or cinnamon-sugar into a small brown paper bag. While the doughnuts are still warm, shake them in the bag to coat them completely with sugar.

St. Joseph's Day Bread

MAKES 2 LOAVES

This subtly sweet bread makes a delicious breakfast and is a good "keeper," meaning that it also makes great leftovers.

1½ cups warm water
2 packages active dry yeast
2 tablespoons vegetable shortening and extra for the bowl
1 tablespoon sugar
1 tablespoon vegetable oil
2 teaspoons salt
4 to 4½ cups all-purpose flour plus extra for the work surface
1 egg, lightly beaten with a fork

1. In a large mixing bowl, combine the warm water, yeast, shortening, sugar, oil, and salt. Let stand for 5 minutes.

2. Into a large mixing bowl, sift 2½ cups flour. Add the yeast mixture to the flour; beat until well blended. Stir in enough of the remaining flour to form a stiff dough. You probably won't use the entire amount of flour.

3. Lightly flour a large work surface or wooden board. Turn out the dough onto the work surface. Knead in more of the flour to form a stiff, smooth dough. Shape into a ball. Place in a large greased bowl. Turn the dough in the bowl to coat with grease. Cover and set aside to rise.

KNEAD DOUGH

4. When the dough has doubled in size, punch it down and divide it into 6 equal pieces. Cover and allow to rest for 10 minutes.

PUNCH DOWN THE DOUGH

5. Roll each piece of dough into a foot-long rope. Braid 3 of the ropes together to form a long braid. Place on a lightly greased baking sheet. Repeat with the remaining 3 ropes of dough to form a second braid. Place on the greased baking sheet. Cover with a clean, damp kitchen towel and let rise until double in size.

6. Preheat the oven to 400°F. Remove the damp towel from the loaves. Brush the tops of the loaves with the beaten egg. Bake for about 25 minutes or until golden brown. Remove the loaves from the baking sheet and cool on a wire rack.

St. Joseph's Day Pastries

MAKES 1 DOZEN

These puffy, tender cream puffs are filled with sweetened ricotta cheese. If you are in a hurry, omit the cheese filling and fill them with whipped or instant vanilla pudding cream instead.

For the cream puffs:
1 cup water
½ cup (1 stick) unsalted butter
½ teaspoon salt
1 cup all-purpose flour
4 eggs
1 tablespoon granulated sugar
Grated rind of ½ lemon

For the filling:
1 cup ricotta cheese
4 tablespoons mini semisweet chocolate chips
4 tablespoons sugar
1 teaspoon vanilla extract

For the topping:
½ cup confectioners' sugar

1. Preheat the oven to 375°F. Line a baking sheet with parchment paper.

2. *Make the cream puffs:* In a 2-quart saucepan, combine the water, butter, and salt. Bring to a boil over medium-high heat. Remove from the heat and add the flour all at once. Stir it very well.

3. Reduce the heat to low and return the saucepan to the heat. Continue to beat for about 5 minutes, until the mixture begins to form a ball. There will be a very slight film on the bottom of the pan. Remove from the heat. Let cool for 5 minutes.

4. Add the eggs, one at a time, and beat vigorously until the dough is smooth after each addition. Add the granulated sugar and the lemon rind, and mix until very smooth.

5. Spoon the dough in large, rounded tablespoonsful 2 inches apart onto the prepared baking sheet. Mound them so they are slightly higher in the center.

6. Bake for 30 minutes, until puffy and browned. Turn off the oven. Leave the cream puffs in the oven for another 10 minutes to dry out.

7. *Make the filling:* In a medium mixing bowl, with an electric mixer set on medium speed, beat the ricotta until smooth. Stir in the chocolate chips, sugar, and vanilla. Mix very well.

8. With a sharp serrated knife, split each cream puff in half. Remove any sticky dough inside. When you are ready to serve, spoon filling into the cavity of each cream puff. Replace the tops.

9. Measure the confectioners' sugar into a sifter. Carefully sift it over the top of each cream puff.

CREAM PUFF

SERRATED KNIFE

CUT WITH SERRATED KNIFE

FIT TOGETHER

◁– PUFF TOP

◀FILLING

◁— PUFF BOTTOM

Chocolatiest Chocolate Biscotti

MAKES 5 DOZEN

Biscotti are Italian cookies that are baked not once but twice. Crisp and crunchy, they're great for dunking in milk. My friend Nick Malgieri, who is in charge of the baking program at the Institute of Culinary Education, gave me this recipe from his book Cookies Unlimited *(HarperCollins). The biscotti have chunks of dark and milk chocolate, so they are perfect for chocoholics.*

1¾ cups all-purpose flour plus extra for the work surface and your hands

⅔ cup unsweetened cocoa powder

2 teaspoons baking powder

Pinch of salt

1¼ cups sugar

6 ounces semisweet chocolate, cut into ¼-inch pieces

6 ounces milk chocolate, cut into ¼-inch pieces

4 eggs

1 teaspoon vanilla extract

1. Position a rack in the middle of the oven. Preheat the oven to 325°F. Line a large baking sheet with parchment paper.

2. In a large mixing bowl, combine the flour, cocoa powder, baking powder, and salt; stir to mix. Stir in the sugar. Add the chocolate to the flour mixture.

3. In a medium bowl, beat the eggs with a wire whisk. Add the vanilla and beat briefly. With a large rubber spatula, stir the eggs into the flour mixture to form a dough.

4. On a lightly floured work surface, press the dough together. It will be sticky. Put some flour on your hands and on the work surface, but don't add any more flour to the dough. Divide the dough in half. With a rolling pin, roll each half into a log 14 to 18 inches long.

5. Place the logs on the baking sheet and make sure they're not too close to each other. Press down gently with the palm of your hand to flatten the logs. If there is any excess flour, use a dry brush to remove it.

6. Bake the logs for about 30 minutes, until they have risen and spread to double their original width. They are done when they feel firm to the touch of your fingertip. Cool the logs on the baking sheet.

7. Reset the oven racks so that they are in the upper and lower thirds of the oven. With a sharp serrated knife, cut the baked logs diagonally into ¼- to ½-inch-thick slices. Return the biscotti to the baking sheet, cut side down. Bake for 15 to 20 minutes. They are done when they are dry and crisp.

8. Store the cooled biscotti between sheets of parchment or waxed paper in a container with a tightly fitting lid.

Cornmeal Butter Cookies

MAKES 20 COOKIES

(Paste di meliga)

This is another recipe from Nick Malgieri's book Cookies Unlimited. *These cookies have a delicate flavor and a coarse texture. For the prettiest cookies, pipe the dough into double S curves. If you don't have a pastry bag, you can drop the dough from a teaspoon onto the prepared baking sheets.*

10 tablespoons (1¼
  sticks) unsalted
  butter, at room
  temperature
½ cup sugar
1 teaspoon vanilla
  extract
2 large egg yolks
1 cup all-purpose flour
⅔ cup stone-ground
  yellow cornmeal

1. Position racks in the upper and lower thirds of the oven. Preheat the oven to 325°F. Line 2 baking sheets with parchment paper.

2. In a large mixing bowl, with an electric mixer set on medium speed, beat the butter, sugar, and vanilla for 5 minutes or until soft and fluffy. Add the egg yolks, one at a time, beating until smooth after each addition. With a large rubber spatula, stir in the flour and the cornmeal.

3. Using a pastry bag fitted with a ½-inch star tube, pipe the dough onto the prepared pans in double S curves about 2½ inches long. Leave about 1½ inches of space between the cookies as these will spread out quite a bit during baking.

4. Bake the cookies for 15 minutes or until firm and very light golden.

5. Slide the parchment papers from the pans onto racks to cool. Store the cooled cookies between sheets of wax paper in a container with a tightly fitting lid.

CORNMEAL BUTTER COOKIES

Purim

O f all the Jewish holidays, Purim may be the happiest. Marked by merriment, it features parades, masquerades, and a good time for everyone. Children and adults often dress up in costumes and may participate in carnivals at their synagogue.

Purim recalls the triumph of the Jewish people over Haman in Persia during the fifth century. According to Bible stories, Haman was a deceitful man who took advantage of King Ahasuerus to seize enormous power for himself. When King Ahasuerus ordered everyone to bow down to Haman, Mordechai, a Jew who once had saved the king's life, refused to do so. Furious, Haman convinced the king that all Jewish people were disloyal. He wanted them killed.

What Haman and the king didn't know was that the king's wife, Queen Esther, was Jewish and also a cousin of Mordechai. When the queen learned of Haman's plot, she told the king that she was Jewish and that Haman planned to have not just her but all her people killed. The king, realizing that Haman was a danger, ordered him hanged on the very gallows that was intended for Mordechai.

The day upon which Haman died became a celebration of life by rich and poor alike. People began to exchange food, especially sweets, and to give money to the poor.

Queen Esther, Purim's heroine, happened to be a vegetarian, so many foods served on this day contain seeds, grains, and fruits. The seed most closely associated with Purim by Jews in the United States is the poppy seed, which has a rich, nutty flavor. In Yiddish, poppy seeds are called *mohn*, and they have been used to flavor food since early biblical times.

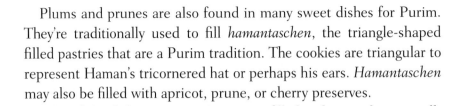

Plums and prunes are also found in many sweet dishes for Purim. They're traditionally used to fill *hamantaschen*, the triangle-shaped filled pastries that are a Purim tradition. The cookies are triangular to represent Haman's tricornered hat or perhaps his ears. *Hamantaschen* may also be filled with apricot, prune, or cherry preserves.

A lot of the dishes eaten on Purim are filled with something, recalling the many secrets and surprises that characterize the Purim story. *Rugelach,* another filled dessert, are delicious little cookies made with cream cheese pastry. They are eaten not just on Purim but on other special occasions.

Grandma's Poppy Seed Hamantaschen

The filling in these tender little pastries is rich and satisfying, thanks to the poppy seeds, walnuts, and raisins.

For the filling:
½ cup poppy seeds
½ cup milk
I tablespoon unsalted butter
¼ cup golden raisins
¼ cup chopped walnuts
I tablespoon light corn syrup
½ teaspoon vanilla extract

For the dough:
½ cup (I stick) unsalted butter, at room temperature
½ cup sugar
3 eggs
Grated rind of I orange
2 cups flour plus extra for the dough and the work surface
I ½ teaspoons baking powder
¼ teaspoon salt
Vegetable shortening for greasing the pan

1. *Make the filling:* In a heavy saucepan, combine the poppy seeds, milk, butter, raisins, walnuts, and corn syrup; bring to a boil. Stir over medium heat for 2 or 3 minutes or until thickened. Remove from the heat and allow to cool for 15 minutes. Stir in the vanilla.

2. *Make the dough:* In a large bowl, with an electric mixer set on medium speed, beat the butter and sugar for 2 minutes or until fluffy. Beat in 2 eggs and the orange rind.

3. Into a separate bowl, sift the 2 cups flour, baking powder, and salt. Add the flour mixture to the butter mixture and mix well; set aside.

4. Preheat the oven to 375°F. Line 2 baking sheets with foil and lightly grease them with vegetable shortening.

5. Divide the dough into 4 equal parts. Sprinkle each lightly with flour. Roll out each piece on a floured work surface. The dough should be about ¼ inch thick. With a round cookie cutter, cut the dough into 2½-inch rounds. If the dough seems sticky, refrigerate, wrapped in plastic, for 10 minutes and then roll out. Spoon about a teaspoon of poppy seed filling into the center of each round. Fold the edges of the rounds

over the filling. Try not to let the filling spill onto the dough. Pinch and shape into triangles, leaving the filling exposed in the center. Place on the prepared baking sheets.

6. Lightly beat the remaining egg in a small bowl and brush over the tops of the cookies. Bake the cookies for 15 to 20 minutes, until golden brown. Remove to a rack and cool.

Apricot-Pineapple Filling

MAKES 3 CUPS

This is a delicious alternative to the poppy seed filling. Just substitute this for the poppy seed filling and follow the preceding recipe. Spread leftovers on warm bread or on pound cake.

2 cups apricot-pineapple preserves
½ cup shredded coconut
½ cup chopped walnuts
I teaspoon grated lemon rind

In a large bowl, combine all the ingredients; mix well. Use to fill *hamantaschen* (see preceding recipe).

Sour Cream- Poppy Seed Cookies

Here's another recipe that uses poppy seeds. These cookies are tender and delicious, and very easy to make.

Cooking spray for greasing the pans
2 cups all-purpose flour
1½ teaspoons baking powder
½ teaspoon salt
½ cup (1 stick) unsalted butter, at room temperature
1¼ cups sugar (divided)
2 eggs
1 teaspoon vanilla extract
1 cup sour cream
⅓ cup white grape juice
2 ounces poppy seeds

1. Preheat the oven to 350°F. Line 2 baking sheets with foil. Lightly spray them with cooking spray.

2. Into a medium mixing bowl, sift the flour, baking powder, and salt; set aside.

3. In a large mixing bowl, with an electric mixer set on medium speed, beat the butter and 1 cup of the sugar for 2 minutes or until light and fluffy. Add the eggs, then the vanilla and the sour cream; beat for 1 minute. Add half the flour mixture to the creamed mixture, then half the white grape juice. Beat for 2 minutes on medium speed. Add the remaining flour, then the remaining white grape juice, and beat until blended. Stir in the poppy seeds. Allow the dough to rest for 15 minutes.

4. Spoon the dough by the heaping teaspoon about 2 inches apart onto the prepared baking sheets. Bake for 8 to 10 minutes, until the cookies are lightly browned. Remove the cookies from the oven and sprinkle with the remaining ¼ cup sugar. Place under the broiler for 20 seconds or until golden. Remove cookies to a rack to cool.

Queen Esther's Sephardic Cookie Rings

These sweet, crisp rings are a traditional favorite in Syria, Turkey, and India. They may be served on the Sabbath as well as at Purim. The rings symbolize Queen Esther's jewelry. These will keep for a week at room temperature, or they may be frozen.

4 cups all-purpose flour
½ teaspoon salt
1 tablespoon baking powder
4 eggs
1 cup sugar
1 cup vegetable oil
1 teaspoon vanilla extract

1. Into a large bowl, sift the flour, salt, and baking powder. In a large mixing bowl, with an electric mixer set on medium speed, beat the eggs for 1 minute. Add the sugar, oil, and vanilla and beat for 1 or 2 minutes. Stir in the sifted flour to make a soft dough. Cover and refrigerate for 30 minutes.

2. Position a rack in the center of the oven. Preheat the oven to 350°F. Line 3 baking sheets with parchment paper.

3. Roll the dough into ½-inch-thick ropes. Cut the ropes into 6-inch lengths, bring the ends together to form rings, and pinch to seal. Place the rings about 1 inch apart on the baking sheets.

4. Bake the rings for about 20 minutes, until firm and golden but not browned. Transfer to a rack, using a spatula, and allow to cool completely.

EGGS BROWN OR WHITE

Peter Rabbit's Carrot Pudding

SERVES 6

Even if you never liked carrots before, this recipe will change your mind. It is adapted from a recipe given to me by a Jewish cook when I worked many years ago as a reporter for a New Jersey newspaper. My two- and four-year-olds liked it immediately.

Vegetable oil for
  greasing the mold
¼ cup plain bread
  crumbs
2 eggs
¾ cup butter, at room
  temperature
¾ cup firmly packed
  brown sugar
1 cup grated carrots
2 teaspoons hot water
½ tablespoon freshly
  squeezed lemon juice
1½ cups all-purpose
  flour
½ teaspoon baking soda
1 teaspoon baking
  powder

1. Preheat the oven to 375°F. Lightly grease a 1- or 1½-quart baking dish with oil. Sprinkle the bottom of the dish with the bread crumbs.

2. In a large mixing bowl, with an electric mixer set on medium speed, beat the eggs for 2 minutes. Add the butter and brown sugar and beat for 1 minute. Stir in the carrots, the water, and lemon juice.

3. Into a medium bowl, sift the flour, baking soda, and baking powder. Add the flour mixture to the carrot mixture and beat until blended. Scrape the mixture into the prepared baking dish.

4. Bake the pudding for 40 to 45 minutes, until the top is golden brown. Serve warm, and be sure to refrigerate any leftovers.

Almond Macaroons

MAKES 2½ DOZEN

Macaroons are chewy or crunchy little cookies traditionally made with almond paste or almonds, plus egg whites and sugar. I love all kinds, but this version, flavored with a little bit of cardamom, is especially good. If you haven't ever tasted cardamom, you will come to love this aromatic spice. It is native to India and grows in other tropical areas, too, like Asia and South America.

Cooking spray and flour for coating the baking sheets
3 cups finely ground blanched almonds
1¼ cups sugar
3 egg whites
½ teaspoon ground cardamom
¼ cup slivered almonds

1. Preheat the oven to 325°F. Lightly spray 2 baking sheets with cooking spray and dust them with a little flour.

2. Combine the almonds and the sugar in a food processor and process till blended. Transfer the mixture to a large bowl. Stir in the egg whites and the cardamom. You should have a pasty dough.

3. Form cookies by dropping dough from a teaspoon about an inch apart onto the prepared baking sheets. Place a slivered almond on top of each cookie.

4. Bake for 10 minutes or until golden brown. With a spatula remove the cookies from the baking sheets, and allow to cool completely. These will keep for 3 or 4 days at room temperature, and you may also freeze them.

Poppy Seed and Almond Cake

A lush chocolate icing dresses up this moist, homey cake, which has ground almonds and chopped apple in addition to the poppy seeds.

Oil for greasing the
   baking pan
2 medium apples,
   preferably Granny
   Smith
6 eggs, separated
7 tablespoons superfine
   sugar
Scant cup finely ground
   blanched almonds
Scant cup poppy seeds
1 recipe Chocolate Icing
   (see following recipe)

1. Lightly oil a 9½-inch round springform pan. Line the bottom with parchment paper.

2. Peel, core, and grate the apples. Use your hands to squeeze out any juice. Set aside.

3. In a medium bowl, with an electric mixer set on medium speed, beat the yolks and the sugar for several minutes, until thick and lemon colored. Stir in the almonds and the poppy seeds. Add the chopped apple and stir to combine.

4. In a separate bowl, beat the egg whites on high speed until they form stiff peaks. Gently fold the egg whites into the egg yolk and sugar mixture. Scrape the batter into the prepared pan.

5. Bake for 25 to 30 minutes, until firm. Cool the cake in the pan for 10 minutes. Loosen the springform part of the pan. Transfer the cake to a serving platter. When it is cool, frost with Chocolate Icing.

Chocolate Icing

¼ **pound semisweet chocolate**
3 **tablespoons milk**
¼ **cup (½ stick) unsalted butter, at room temperature**
1½ **to 2 cups confectioners' sugar**

1. Break the chocolate into small pieces. Place the chocolate in a small glass bowl. Heat in the microwave oven on high for 45 seconds. Stir and return the bowl to the microwave; cook for another 20 seconds.

2. When the chocolate has melted, beat in the milk and butter with an electric mixer set on medium speed until well blended. Beat in 1½ cups of confectioners' sugar. Beat in more if necessary to make the icing spreadable.

3. When the icing is thin enough to spread, pour it over the cake. Set the cake aside until the icing hardens.

Passover

Every spring, Jewish people celebrate Passover, the eight-day Festival of Freedom, which commemorates the Exodus of the Israelites from slavery in Egypt. Pharaoh, Egypt's ruler, wouldn't let the Jewish people go, so God sent ten plagues upon the Egyptians. After the last plague, Pharaoh finally decided to let the Jews go. Leaving in a tremendous hurry, the Jews did not have time to let their bread rise. To acknowledge this hardship, Jews eat matzo, which is unleavened bread, each Passover.

The holiday really begins the night before, when everyone in the household searches for any remaining *chametz*, which is food that may not be eaten during this holiday. A special family meal, called a "seder," is celebrated. The Passover table is festive and beautiful to look at. There might be an ivory-colored tablecloth and napkins, a bouquet of spring flowers, and candles. Everyone in the family participates in the ceremony, which involves readings and prayers from a book known as the *Haggadah*.

Each food on the seder plate has special meaning. There is a roasted egg that recalls the time when offerings were made in the temple in Jerusalem and also symbolizes new life. Haroset, a fruit and nut mixture often flavored with cinnamon, stands for the mortar and bricks the Israelites used to build pyramids when they were slaves in Egypt. The red wine in the haroset reminds the Jewish people that God parted the Red Sea during the Exodus from Egypt. There are bitter herbs, such as horseradish, which stand for the bitterness of slavery in Egypt. Horseradish eaten with haroset in a matzo sandwich shows the two sides of life: sweet and bitter. Parsley, which stands for life and hope, is dipped in saltwater to recall the salty tears of the slaves. And a burnt portion of a leg of lamb represents the paschal offering.

When it comes to dessert, Passover is a time to be creative. Since baking soda and baking powder aren't permitted, cakes must be leavened in other ways. Eggs are often used to leaven baked goods because when they are separated, and the whites whipped to stiff peaks, they yield satisfying cakes and tortes. It's also common at Passover to find cakes made with ground nuts and with fruit such as oranges. Depending on where in the world you live, a Passover dessert might be flavored with rosewater or vanilla.

Passover Chocolate Cake

SERVES 8

If you like a really chocolaty dessert, top this with chocolate sauce. If you prefer creamy fillings, split the cake in half and fill and frost it with sweetened whipped cream.

One piece of advice about handling eggs. Eggs that are at room temperature hold triple the air of chilled eggs, meaning they can be beaten to a greater volume. So be sure to remove the eggs from the refrigerator half an hour before you start mixing up a cake so they will be at the optimum temperature. If you forget or don't have time, put the eggs in a bowl of warm water for two minutes instead.

Oil and fine matzo meal
    for coating the pan
1¼ cups whole blanched
    almonds
⅔ cup sugar
5 eggs, separated
1¼ teaspoons vanilla
    extract
6 ounces semisweet
    chocolate, finely
    chopped
Pinch of salt
3 tablespoons cocoa
    powder for topping

1. Preheat the oven to 350°F. Oil a 9 by 3-inch spring-form pan and dust it with matzo meal.

2. Place the almonds on an ungreased baking sheet. Toast them in the oven for about 10 minutes, stirring occasionally. Set aside to cool.

3. In the work bowl of a food processor, grind the almonds with half the sugar. Remove from work bowl when the nuts are very finely chopped.

4. In a large mixing bowl, with an electric mixer set on medium speed, beat the egg yolks with the vanilla and the remaining sugar for 2 minutes. When the batter is creamy, add the nuts and chocolate and beat for 30 seconds.

5. Wash the beater and use it, set on low speed, to beat the egg whites and salt in another mixing bowl. When the whites are foamy, turn the speed to high and beat until soft peaks form.

6. With a spatula, fold one third of the egg whites into the chocolate mixture. Add the remaining whites in two batches, folding very gently. Spoon the batter into the prepared springform pan.

RUBBER SPATULA

7. Bake for 30 to 35 minutes. When the cake is done, it will still be a little moist in the middle. Cool for 10 minutes, then gently loosen the springform part of the pan. Allow the cake to cool completely. Measure the cocoa powder into a sifter and sift it over the top of the cake.

Walnut and Apple Haroset

This kind of haroset, a fruit and nut mixture seasoned with cinnamon, is eaten by Ashkenazi Jews from Eastern Europe. You can chop the nuts in a food processor or else pound them by hand, using a mortar and pestle. But don't chop them too finely because you want the consistency to be chunky. This is good spread on little pieces of matzo.

1 lemon
2½ cups peeled and chopped apple
2 cups shelled walnuts, coarsely chopped
¾ teaspoon ground cinnamon
½ cup grape juice
2 teaspoons sugar

1. Grate the lemon rind with a fine grater and measure out 1 teaspoon of the grated rind. Reserve the rest for another use.

2. In a large bowl, combine the grated lemon rind, chopped apple, walnuts, cinnamon, grape juice, and sugar; stir until well mixed. Cover and refrigerate until serving time.

WALNUTS

← MORTAR AND PESTLE

Passover Butter Cookies

This is a tender, rich cookie to enjoy anytime. If you follow the Jewish dietary laws, this counts as a dairy dessert during Passover.

1½ cups sugar
½ cup (1 stick) unsalted butter, at room temperature
4 eggs
2 cups matzo cake meal
1 cup chopped nuts

1. In a large mixing bowl, with an electric mixer set on medium speed, beat the sugar and butter for 2 minutes or until fluffy. Add the eggs and beat well.

2. Stir in the cake meal and the nuts. Stir very well with a wooden spoon. Roll into a rope that is about 1½ inches in diameter. Refrigerate for several hours.

3. Preheat the oven to 350°F. Cut the roll of dough crosswise into ¼-inch-thick slices. Bake the cookies 2 inches apart on an ungreased baking sheet for 15 minutes or until golden. Remove from the baking sheet with a spatula and cool completely.

Passover Brownies

These are rich and satisfying. If you don't like nuts, you can leave them out. Or add chocolate chips instead.

Kosher for Passover
  vegetable shortening
  for greasing pan
2 cups sugar
½ cup kosher for
  Passover vegetable
  shortening
4 eggs
½ cup kosher for
  Passover cocoa powder
¼ teaspoon kosher salt
½ cup water
1 cup matzo cake meal
⅓ cup potato starch
1 cup chopped nuts

1. Preheat the oven to 350°F. Lightly grease a 9 by 13-inch baking pan with the vegetable shortening.

2. In a large bowl, with an electric mixer set on medium speed, beat the sugar and shortening for 2 minutes or until light and fluffy. Add the eggs and beat well. Add the cocoa and beat for 30 seconds. Add the remaining ingredients, except for the nuts, and beat until well combined.

3. Stir in the nuts. Scrape the batter into the prepared pan. Bake for 25 to 30 minutes, until a cake tester inserted into the center comes out clean. Remove from the oven, cool, and cut into 24 bars.

☆Orange and Nut Passover Cake

This simple, unfrosted cake has a pleasant, citrusy flavor. For maximum volume, be sure your beaters are very clean before whipping the egg whites.

Oil and matzo meal for coating the pan
1 large orange
6 eggs
1¾ cups sugar
¾ cup ground almonds
1½ cups chopped walnuts

1. Preheat the oven to 350°F. Lightly oil a 9-inch springform pan. Sprinkle the bottom of the pan with matzo meal.

2. Grate the orange rind with a fine grater. Squeeze the juice into a small bowl. Set aside.

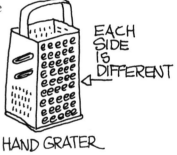

EACH SIDE IS DIFFERENT

HAND GRATER

3. Separate the eggs into 2 large mixing bowls. With an electric mixer set on medium speed, beat the yolks and the sugar for several minutes, until pale yellow. Stir in the ground almonds. Stir in the orange juice, the orange rind, and the walnuts; beat 1 minute.

4. Wash the beaters very well and dry them. Beat the egg whites on high speed for 2 minutes or until stiff peaks form. Gently fold the nut mixture into the beaten egg whites, being careful not to stir too vigorously (or the cake might not be as light as it should be).

5. Spoon and scrape the batter into the prepared pan. Bake for about 1 hour to 1 hour and 10 minutes, until a tester inserted into the center comes out clean.

6. Cool the cake in the pan for 10 minutes. Gently remove the springform part of the pan and allow the cake to cool completely before serving.

Passover Raspberry-Jam Cookies

These little morsels are like those old-fashioned thumbprint cookies. You can pre-pare the dough in advance and store it in the refrigerator for a couple of days. You can also freeze the dough for up to one month. Thaw it in the refrigerator overnight. And if you prefer strawberry or apricot jam to raspberry, feel free to make a substitution.

Cooking spray for the
    baking sheets
1 large orange
1 cup sugar
1 cup (2 sticks) unsalted
    butter, at room
    temperature
3 egg yolks
2 scant cups matzo cake
    meal
3 tablespoons potato
    starch
Pinch of salt
1/2 cup seedless
    raspberry jam

1. Preheat the oven to 375°F. Lightly spray 2 baking sheets with cooking spray.

2. Using a fine metal grater, grate the orange rind. Measure out 2½ teaspoons. Squeeze all the juice from the orange. Measure out 2 tablespoons of juice. (Drink any remaining juice.) Set aside the grated orange zest and juice.

3. In a large mixing bowl, with an electric mixer set on medium speed, beat the sugar and butter for 2 minutes or until smooth and creamy. Add the egg yolks and beat for 1 minute. Stir in the cake meal, potato starch, salt, the orange zest, and the 2 tablespoons juice. Mix until creamy.

4. Shape the dough into 1-inch balls. Place the balls 1 inch apart on the baking sheet. Make a little indentation in the center of each cookie by pressing on the cookie with your thumb.

5. Bake the cookies for 7 minutes, until they are firm. Remove cookies from oven. Spoon ¼ teaspoon of jam into each indentation. Return the cookies to the oven for 1 minute.

6. Remove the cookies from the oven. With a spatula, transfer the cookies from the baking sheet to a rack. Let them cool completely before storing them in a tin.

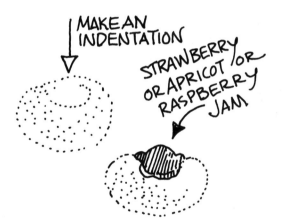

MAKE AN INDENTATION

STRAWBERRY OR APRICOT OR RASPBERRY JAM

Passover Apple Crisp

SERVES 6

A holiday variation on a classic dessert, this is best served warm. It comes from my friend Susan. Years ago, her son Adam (who is now in college) attended a nursery school that assembled a little collection of easy Passover recipes for its pupils.

Margarine for greasing the baking pan
6 apples
½ cup sugar
½ teaspoon salt
2 cups matzo farfel
¾ cup brown sugar
¾ teaspoon ground cinnamon
½ cup (1 stick) margarine, at room temperature

1. Preheat the oven to 350°F. Lightly grease a 9-inch round cake pan with margarine.

2. Peel, core, and slice the apples. Toss the apple slices with sugar and salt.

3. Slightly moisten the matzo farfel with a little water; drain. In a bowl, crumble together the matzo farfel, brown sugar, cinnamon, and margarine. When the mixture is nice and crumbly, spread over the apples.

4. Bake for 45 minutes, or until the top is golden brown.

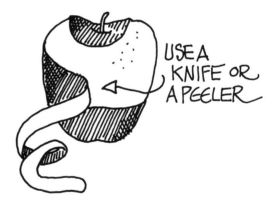

USE A KNIFE OR A PEELER

Light as a Cloud Chocolate Meringues

This recipe is also from my friend Susan, who used to make these delicious cookies with her sons, Adam and Jeff. You can use whatever nuts you like. My kids love the cookies made with pecans.

Vegetable shortening for greasing the baking sheets
1 (6-ounce) package chocolate chips
2 egg whites
Dash of salt
½ cup sugar
½ teaspoon white vinegar
½ teaspoon vanilla extract
¾ cup chopped nuts

1. Preheat the oven to 350°F. Lightly grease some baking sheets.

2. In the top of a double boiler set over simmering water, melt the chocolate chips. Set aside to cool.

3. In a mixing bowl, with an electric mixer set on high speed, beat the egg whites and the salt. When soft peaks form, start to gradually add the sugar. Add the vinegar and vanilla and beat until stiff peaks form. Fold in the chocolate with a spatula. Fold in the chopped nuts.

4. Using a scant teaspoon of dough for each cookie, form cookies on the prepared baking sheets. Space them 1 inch apart. Bake for 8 to 10 minutes. Remove the cookies from the oven and transfer them to a rack to cool.

Easter

*I*t puzzled me when my mother used to tell us that Easter was a more important holiday than Christmas. It was definitely more low key, and though we got candy, the jelly beans and chocolate bunnies didn't begin to compare with the gifts and the excitement of Christmas.

As I got older, though, I came to learn that my mother (as usual) had been right. Christmas is about the birth of Jesus, but Easter celebrates his resurrection from the dead, and it is an incredibly joyous occasion. After dying a terrible death, the fact that He had actually risen from the dead to sit at the right hand of God the Father reaffirms the Christian faith and helps worshipers to realize how much God loves them.

The joyous occasion of Easter is preceded by a reflective and somber six-week period known as Lent. During Lent, to commemorate the forty days that Jesus spent praying in the wilderness before his death, Catholics deny themselves treats of all kinds. In my family, we children gave up dessert, ice cream, candy, or chips, depending upon how much we felt like sacrificing. Of course, there were always a few sly ones among my younger siblings who tried to give up spinach, or string beans, or meat loaf. My mother saw to it that these foods were still eaten by everyone in the household.

As schoolchildren, we used to go to Mass in Lent every morning at seven A.M., before school. We ate very little meat, and every Friday night, we were faced with a fish dinner, which I despised.

But things started looking up toward the end of the Lenten season. We hard-boiled eggs and decorated them in bright colors. We chose the pastel-colored dresses we would wear to church on Easter and scrubbed the house from top to bottom. By Palm Sunday, I always felt that we were nearing the end of a too-long period of mourning.

Palm Sunday, exactly a week before Easter, recalls the day that Jesus and his followers went to Jerusalem on a donkey to celebrate Passover. (Jesus and his followers were Jews.) Because the crowds that gathered waved palm branches to welcome him, this is the day that palms are blessed in churches and handed out to the congregation to take home.

Good Friday, just two days before Easter, marks the day Jesus died on the cross. We always stayed in church for a good part of this day, and we remained silent on that day from noon to three P.M., to commemorate the three-hour period Jesus hung on the cross.

On the night before Easter, once we were old enough, we were permitted to attend midnight Mass and to stay up way past our bedtime. Then, in the morning, we woke up and had to hunt for our baskets of candy. Every year the Easter bunny got more ingenious about where he hid them. Once I found mine in the oven, which thankfully my mother had not yet turned on to bake her Easter dinner.

My children and I not only go to Mass Easter Sunday morning to honor Jesus as our savior and to celebrate his eternal life, but we host a big family dinner for all the aunts, uncles, grandparents, and cousins. Before dessert, we have an Easter egg hunt for all the younger cousins. Sometimes instead of foil-wrapped chocolate eggs or tiny toys, I fill a few of the plastic eggs with little pieces of paper that say "You win a chocolate bunny" or "You have to do the dishes" and slip these to the grown-ups in the crowd. There is always a lot of silliness as everyone tries to give away the eggs instructing the recipient to do some chores!

Italians celebrate the holiday with a variety of special breads and cakes. One Easter cheese bread is baked in terra-cotta flowerpots; another is shaped like a dove and topped with sugar and toasted almonds. Italians also prepare a cheesecake with a crust made with

wheat berries and a filling made with fresh ricotta cheese and, often, candied orange peel. Some cooks also make a sweet ricotta pie, which is even easier to make than a cheesecake.

Russian cooks have their own special Easter confections, including a rich, creamy, crustless no-bake cheesecake called *paskha*, and *kulich*, a cylindrical dome-shaped bread that contains toasted sliced almonds, candied fruit, and raisins. In Greece, cooks make shortbread cookies called *koulourakia*, which can be shaped into rings, pretzels, sticks, or wreaths.

Lenten Hot Cross Buns

MAKES 20 BUNS

These aren't too sweet, which makes them a good alternative to bagels in the morning. If you don't like raisins you can leave them out, but they taste especially good in these golden buns. You'll know the milk and water are the right temperature when they feel warm to your touch.

Butter for greasing the
  bowl and baking pan
¾ cup milk
1 package active dry
  yeast
¼ cup warm water
⅓ cup sugar
1 teaspoon salt
¼ cup (½ stick) butter,
  at room temperature
2 eggs
3¼ cups (or more) all-
  purpose flour plus
  extra for work surface
¾ teaspoon ground
  cinnamon
½ teaspoon ground
  nutmeg
½ cup raisins

1. Lightly grease a large mixing bowl with butter. Pour the milk into a small saucepan and heat it over very low heat until it is warm to the touch. In a small bowl, stir the yeast into the water. Set it aside for 5 minutes, until the yeast has dissolved.

2. In another large mixing bowl, combine the warm milk, sugar, salt, butter, and eggs. Beat with an electric mixer set on medium speed for 1 minute. Add the dissolved yeast and beat for 30 seconds. Beat in 1½ cups of the flour, the cinnamon, and the nutmeg. Cover the bowl with plastic wrap and let it rise for about 1 hour, until double in bulk.

3. Add the remaining flour and stir vigorously to blend it in. You may need to add a bit more flour to make the dough firm. Turn out the dough onto a floured work surface and knead until smooth. Knead in the raisins.

KNEAD DOUGH

Place the dough in the large greased bowl, cover, and allow to rise for 1 hour or until double in bulk.

4. Lightly butter a baking sheet. Punch down the dough. Turn it out onto a lightly floured work surface. Use a rolling pin to roll it out into a ½-inch thick rectangle that is about 14 by 10 inches. Use a round 2½-inch cookie cutter to cut out buns. If you don't

PUNCH DOWN THE DOUGH

have a cookie cutter you can use an inverted drinking glass. Place the buns on the prepared baking sheet.

5. Reroll the dough scraps and cut out more buns until you have used up all the dough. Let the buns rise for 1 hour, or until double in bulk.

6. Flour a pair of scissors. Snip a cross in the top of each bun. Bake the buns for 15 minutes, until they are golden brown. Remove the buns from the oven and use a spatula to transfer them to a rack to cool.

7. If you like, prepare Luscious White Icing and use it to pipe a cross on the top of each bun. When you make the icing, keep the consistency thick so it will hold the shape of a cross.

Easter Bunny Cake

This recipe relies on a cake mix and is super fast, so get hopping!

Nonstick cooking spray for greasing pans
1 (18-ounce) package carrot cake mix
1 cup water
½ cup vegetable oil
3 eggs
2 (12-ounce) cans white frosting
2 cups sweetened flaked coconut
Jelly beans or small gumdrops
Green food color
Shoestring licorice for whiskers

1. Preheat the oven to 350°F. Lightly grease the bottoms only of two 8-inch or 9-inch round cake pans.

2. In a large mixing bowl with an electric mixer set on low speed, beat the cake mix, water, oil, and eggs for 30 seconds. Beat on medium speed for 2 minutes. Pour the batter into the prepared pans.

3. Bake the layers for 25 to 30 minutes, until the center of the cake springs back when you touch it with your finger. Cool the layers in the pans for 10 minutes. Remove from pans. Cool completely, for about 1 hour.

4. To make the body of the bunny, place 1 layer on large baking sheet.

5. Using a sharp knife, cut 2 large ears from remaining layer. The scraps will be a bowtie. Arrange the ears above the body layer and attach with frosting. Arrange scraps to be a bowtie.

6. Frost entire cake. Use jelly beans to decorate the bunny's head with a nose, mouth, and eyes.

7. In a jar with a cover, shake 1 cup of the coconut and 3–5 drops of green food coloring. Place the green-tinted coconut on the bowtie. Place plain coconut on the ears. Decorate with more jelly beans, if desired. Add licorice "whiskers."

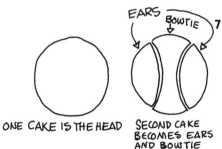

ONE CAKE IS THE HEAD

SECOND CAKE BECOMES EARS AND BOWTIE

BUNNY CAKE READY FOR A FACE!

Italian Easter Pie

Cut this rich pie, which tastes something like cheesecake, into thin slices and serve for dessert. It is also good for breakfast. Be sure to store it in the refrigerator.

For the crust:
½ cup (1 stick) butter
2 eggs
⅓ cup sugar
1½ cups all-purpose
   flour plus extra for
   work surface
Pinch of salt
1 teaspoon baking
   powder

For the filling:
1 lemon
6 eggs
½ cup sugar
½ teaspoon vanilla
   extract
3 cups ricotta cheese

1. *Make the crust:* Place the butter in a small glass bowl; heat in the microwave oven on high a minute or two, stirring once, until it has melted. Remove and set aside to cool.

2. In a medium bowl, with an electric mixer set on medium speed, beat the eggs and the sugar for 2 minutes or until light and fluffy. Add the melted butter and beat 1 minute.

3. Into a medium bowl, sift the flour, salt, and baking powder. Add the dry ingredients to the butter mixture and beat to combine.

4. Turn out the dough onto a lightly floured work surface. Knead in a few more tablespoons of flour so the dough is workable. Divide the dough into two balls. Roll out one half to fit a deep 9-inch pie pan. Roll out the remaining dough and cut it into ½-inch-wide strips.

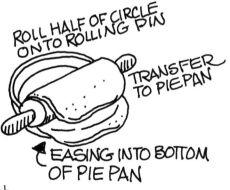

ROLL HALF OF CIRCLE ONTO ROLLING PIN

TRANSFER TO PIE PAN

EASING INTO BOTTOM OF PIE PAN

5. Preheat the oven to 350 degrees.

6. *Make the filling:* Grate the lemon rind using a fine-grater. Cut the lemon in half and squeeze the juice into a small bowl.

7. In a medium mixing bowl, with an electric beater set on medium speed, beat the eggs. Add the sugar, then the lemon juice, lemon rind, and vanilla. Beat for 1 minute. Add the ricotta and beat for 1 minute.

8. Pour the filling into the pie crust. Arrange the dough strips to form a crisscross pattern on top of the pie.

9. Bake for 1 hour or until the center is fairly firm. Turn off the oven but wait 10 minutes before removing the pie. Refrigerate for at least 4 hours before serving.

ITALIAN EASTER PIE

Almond-Topped Creamy Lemon Pie

SERVES 8

This is the easiest pie in the world to make. If you use a prepared graham cracker crust, it's ready in ten minutes. I sometimes garnish it with slivered almonds, but for Easter dessert I like to sprinkle the top with fresh raspberries.

1 (6-ounce) can lemonade concentrate, thawed
1 (14-ounce) can sweetened condensed milk
1 (8-ounce) container Cool Whip, thawed
Juice of 1 lemon
1 (9-inch) graham cracker pie crust
½ cup chopped nuts of your choice for topping

1. In a large mixing bowl, with an electric mixer set on medium speed, beat the lemonade, sweetened condensed milk, Cool Whip, and lemon juice until thoroughly blended.

2. Spoon the filling into the graham cracker crust, mounding it slightly in the center. Sprinkle with nuts, berries, or colored sprinkles. Cover with plastic wrap and refrigerate for at least 1 hour before serving. Store the pie in the refrigerator.

Carrot-Walnut Bunny Bread

MAKES 4 BUNNIES, 2 BIG, 2 SMALL

This bread is very good spread with softened butter or cream cheese. If you like you can just make 2 very large bunnies, and remember—sometimes the dough rises too high, in which case you'll have very chubby bunnies—but they'll still taste good.

4½ cups plus 1 cup unsifted all-purpose flour
2 cups grated raw carrots, at room temperature
¾ cup chopped walnuts
2 tablespoons sugar
2 teaspoons salt
2 packages active dry yeast
1 cup water
⅔ cup milk
3 tablespoons butter plus extra for greasing the baking sheets
Raisins
1 egg, beaten

1. In a large bowl, combine 4½ cups of the flour, the grated carrots, chopped walnuts, sugar, salt, and active dry yeast; mix well.

2. In a saucepan, combine the water, milk, and 3 tablespoons butter. Heat over low heat just until hot to the touch. Stir into the carrot mixture. Add just enough of the remaining 1 cup flour to form a soft dough.

3. Turn the dough out onto a floured work surface and knead until smooth and elastic. Cover with a bowl and let rest for 10 minutes.

4. With a large sharp knife, divide the dough in half. Set aside one half. Divide the other half into 2 pieces, one twice the size of the other. Divide the larger piece of dough in half and shape one part into a round ball for the body of the bunny. Place this on a greased baking sheet and flatten slightly.

5. Divide the other half into two pieces, one twice the size of the other. Shape this larger piece into a smooth ball and place alongside the "body" as the head. Divide the balance into a small ball of dough for the tail, and

2 tapered rolls for the ears. Press these against the head.

6. Use the remainder of the dough from this half of the recipe to shape a similar smaller bunny. Repeat shaping 2 bunnies from the second ball of the dough. Place these on a second baking sheet. Cover the shaped dough with a towel and place each baking sheet over a large shallow pan half filled with boiling water. Let the dough rise for 40 minutes or until almost doubled in bulk.

7. Preheat the oven to 400°F.

8. Make an indentation in the dough for the ears on each bunny. Press in a raisin for the eyes of each. Brush all over with the beaten egg. Bake for 10 minutes, then reduce the heat to 375 degrees and bake 25 to 30 minutes or until the loaves sound hollow when you tap them. Remove from the baking sheet to a wire rack to cool. The bigger bunnies will take slightly longer to bake than the smaller ones.

Springtime Strawberry Bread

This lovely loaf is nice sliced thinly, with a fruit salad for dessert. You could also spread it with cream cheese and sandwich two slices together. Cut into quarters and serve at an Easter lunch. If you have extra strawberry puree, you can use it in a smoothie.

Butter for greasing the loaf pan
2 eggs
1 pint strawberries
1³⁄₄ cups all-purpose flour
¹⁄₄ teaspoon baking soda
¹⁄₂ teaspoon salt
¹⁄₃ cup butter
²⁄₃ cup sugar

1. Preheat the oven to 350°F. Lightly butter an 8 by 4-inch loaf pan.

2. In a small bowl, beat the eggs with a fork; set aside.

3. Wash and dry the strawberries. Remove the hulls. Put them in a blender and puree them; set aside.

4. Into a medium bowl, sift the flour, baking soda, and salt; set aside.

5. In a large mixing bowl, with an electric mixer set on medium speed, beat the butter with the sugar for 2 minutes or until fluffy. Add the eggs and beat until smooth.

6. Add the flour mixture alternately with 1 cup of the strawberry puree to the butter mixture. Beat 1 minute or until smooth.

7. Spoon and scrape the batter into the prepared pan and bake for 45–60 minutes. The bread is done when a toothpick inserted into the center comes out clean.

8. Cool the bread in the pan for 10 minutes. Run a knife around the edges of the pan to loosen the bread. Turn the bread out onto a rack and allow to cool completely.

Easter Basket Cupcakes

A creamy frosting tops these tender vanilla cupcakes, which make a nice dessert to serve on Easter after a day of pigging out on chocolate.

1¼ cups all-purpose flour
1½ teaspoons baking powder
¼ teaspoon salt
6 tablespoons (¾ stick) unsalted butter, at room temperature
⅔ cup sugar
3 egg yolks
¾ teaspoon vanilla extract
2 cups milk
Finger Licking Buttercream Frosting (see following recipe)
1 cup sweetened flaked coconut
6 or 7 drops green food coloring
Jelly beans

1. Preheat the oven to 350°F. Line 12 muffin cups with paper liners.

2. Into a large mixing bowl, sift the flour, baking powder, and salt; set aside.

3. In a medium mixing bowl, with an electric mixer set on high speed, beat the butter until light and fluffy. Add half the sugar to the butter; beat for 1 minute. Add the remaining sugar and beat 2 minutes. Add the yolks and beat for 1 minute. Add the vanilla, along with half the milk, and beat for 1 minute. Sift half the flour into the batter and add the remaining milk. Beat for 30 seconds. Add the remaining flour. Beat on low speed for 30 seconds.

4. Spoon the batter into the prepared muffin cups. Bake for 18 to 20 minutes. The cupcakes are done when the tops spring back when lightly touched. Cool for 5 minutes in the pan. Remove the cupcakes to a rack to cool completely.

5. To decorate, frost the cupcakes with Buttercream Frosting, using a table knife to spread the frosting evenly.

6. Stir the coconut and green food coloring together in a small bowl. Top each cupcake with some green coconut "grass." Fill the center of each "basket" with jelly beans.

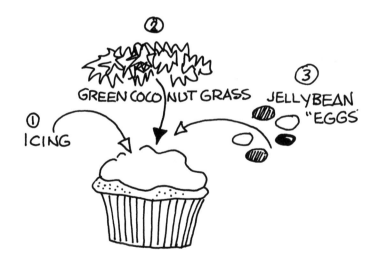

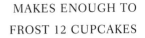

Finger-Licking Buttercream Frosting

¼ cup (½ stick)
 unsalted butter, at
 room temperature
½ of 1-pound box
 confectioners' sugar
⅛ cup milk
1 teaspoon vanilla
 extract
⅛ teaspoon salt

1. In a medium mixing bowl, with an electric beater set on medium speed, beat the butter for 2 minutes.

2. Scrape down the sides of the bowl and add half the sugar. Beat for 1 minute. Add the milk, remaining sugar, vanilla, and salt; beat until smooth.

Strawberry-Rhubarb Crisp

SERVES 6–8

Rhubarb and strawberries go well together in a variety of desserts. My Aunt Puthie makes a fantastic strawberry-rhubarb pie that disappears as soon as she takes it out of the oven. This recipe is much easier than a pie and makes a pretty, homey dessert at Easter. Be sure to discard rhubarb leaves and use only the stalks as rhubarb leaves are poisonous.

For the topping:
½ cup walnuts
1 cup minus 2 tablespoons all-purpose flour
⅓ cup packed light brown sugar
4 teaspoons granulated sugar
Pinch of ground cinnamon
⅓ cup unsalted butter, at room temperature

For the fruit:
½ pint strawberries
1½ pounds rhubarb (no leaves!)
¾ cup granulated sugar
3 tablespoons all-purpose flour

1. *Make the topping:* Preheat the oven to 375°F. Toast the walnuts on a large baking sheet for about 5 minutes, stirring twice. Remove from the oven and set aside.

2. In a medium mixing bowl, stir the flour, light brown sugar, granulated sugar, and cinnamon. Work in the butter with your fingers until the mixture looks crumbly. Chop the walnuts; stir them into the topping.

3. *Prepare the fruit:* Wash, hull, and slice the strawberries. Wash and trim the rhubarb. Cut the rhubarb crosswise into ½-inch-thick slices. You should have about 6 cups.

4. In a large mixing bowl, toss the rhubarb, strawberries, sugar, and flour. Let stand for 10 minutes.

5. Stir the fruit mixture well. Spoon it into a 9-inch pie plate. Smooth out the top. Sprinkle with the topping.

6. Bake on the middle rack of the oven for 45 minutes or until the juices bubble and the topping is golden. Serve warm with whipped cream or vanilla ice cream, if desired.

Cinco de Mayo

Cinco de mayo, which means "May 5th" in Spanish, is becoming more popular than ever here in the United States. Though many people think of this occasion as Mexican Independence Day, it doesn't actually commemorate independence at all but a memorable battle between a large French army and a small Mexican contingent that was fought in 1862 in Puebla, Mexico.

Although the French army was twice the size, this famous battle, under the command of General Ignacio Zaragoza, was won by the determined and courageous Mexican soldiers. Their victory, however sweet, didn't immediately lead to Mexican independence; in fact the French occupation actually increased in intensity after the battle. But just five years after the Battle of Puebla, Mexico won its permanent independence from the French. On June 19, 1867, Mexico's occupation by a foreign country finally came to an end.

Cinco de Mayo celebrations in the United States began gradually, with Hispanic communities starting to mark the occasion with parades featuring colorful floats and special dances. Many people celebrate Cinco de Mayo, which is the primary Mexican-American cultural celebration, by eating a special meal in a Mexican restaurant. Others attend celebrations in parks to watch dancers, listen to music, and eat Mexican food. However you choose to spend May 5, Cinco de Mayo is a great time to think about the courage and valor of a nation that was determined to fight for its freedom no matter what.

On this special day, it's traditional to eat corn tortillas stuffed with meat or cheese, as well as *buñuelos*, which are deep-fried pastries sprinkled with sugar and cinnamon. Here's a selection of Mexican desserts to help you celebrate.

Cornmeal Crunchies

Light and citrusy, these will keep for one week in a tightly covered container.

I large lime
I cup granulated sugar
½ pound (2 sticks)
  unsalted butter, at
  room temperature
I egg
I teaspoon almond
  extract
I teaspoon vanilla
  extract
I cup yellow cornmeal
1½ cups all-purpose
  flour
Flour and cornmeal for
  the work surface
Butter and cornmeal for
  the baking sheets
½ cup confectioners'
  sugar

1. Grate the lime rind with the fine side of a grater; reserve the rind. Squeeze the juice into a small bowl and measure out 2 tablespoons.

2. In a large mixing bowl, with an electric mixer set on medium speed, beat the granulated sugar and the butter. After 1 minute, add the egg. Beat 1 minute. Add the lime juice and the lime rind. Add the almond extract and the vanilla extract; beat well. Add the cornmeal and the flour and beat until combined.

3. Lightly dust a work surface with flour and cornmeal. Place the dough on the work surface and knead it briefly, until you can form it into a fairly firm ball. Chill for 30 minutes.

4. Preheat the oven to 350°F. Lightly butter 2 large baking sheets and sprinkle them with cornmeal.

5. Form walnut-size pieces of the chilled dough into small balls. Place them on the prepared baking sheets about ½ inch apart, and flatten them slightly. Bake for 5 minutes or until the cookies are golden on the bottom. Remove the cookies from the oven.

6. With a spatula, carefully turn the cookies over and return them to the oven for another 5 minutes. Remove the cookies from the oven and cool them on the baking sheets for 3 to 5 minutes. Using a spatula, transfer them to a wire rack.

7. While the cookies are still warm, sift the confectioners' sugar over the tops. Turn the cookies over and sift some sugar onto the other side. Serve the cookies warm or at room temperature.

WHILE STILL WARM

Sopaipillas

Traditionally, sopaipillas, crisp, puffy pastries, are fried, but they taste just as good, and are lower in fat, when they are baked.

Cooking spray for the pan
2 cups all-purpose flour
2 teaspoons baking powder
1 teaspoon salt
2 tablespoons butter
¾ cup water
Flour for the work surface
½ cup honey or 6 tablespoons sugar mixed with 1 teaspoon of ground cinnamon

1. Lightly spray a large baking sheet with cooking spray. Into a large mixing bowl, sift the flour, baking powder, and salt. Cut in the butter with your fingers until the mixture resembles peas. Mix in the water to make a smooth dough.

2. Knead lightly on a floured work surface. Cut the dough into 12 pieces. Shape into balls. Cover and set aside.

3. Preheat the oven to 350°F. Flatten the dough balls slightly. Cut each into a triangle and discard the trimmings. Place on the prepared baking sheet. Bake for 10 to 15 minutes, until golden.

4. While they are warm, either drizzle with honey or sprinkle with cinnamon-sugar.

Tooty Frooty Mango-Strawberry Sauce

SERVES 4

Top rice pudding or vanilla ice cream with this fresh, fruity sauce.

1 cup strawberries
1 mango
2 tablespoons sugar
1 tablespoon orange juice

1. Wash and dry the strawberries. Remove the hulls. Chop them coarsely.

2. Peel the mango. Remove the pit and discard (see note). Coarsely chop the flesh.

3. Place the chopped fruit in a medium stainless-steel saucepan. Add the sugar and the orange juice, and bring to a boil. Reduce the heat and simmer until slightly thickened. This will keep for several days, tightly covered, in the refrigerator.

Note: To prepare a mango, cut it in half, cutting around the pit as well as you can. Score the flesh of each half with a sharp paring knife. Turn the mango as "inside out" as you can and remove the flesh.

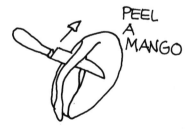

PEEL A MANGO

CUT MANGO ALONG EACH SIDE OF THE FLAT SEED

REMOVE MANGO FLESH

FROM MANGO SHELL

Cinco de Mayo **133**

Pecan-Cinnamon Cookies

MAKES 3½ DOZEN

Store these cookies, which are excellent with ice cream, between layers of waxed paper in an airtight tin or freeze them for up to two months.

1 cup (2 sticks) unsalted butter, at room temperature

1½ cups confectioners' sugar, sifted

1 tablespoon vanilla extract

2 cups all-purpose flour

¼ teaspoon salt

⅔ cup finely ground pecans

1¼ teaspoons ground cinnamon

1. Preheat the oven to 325°F. In a large bowl, with an electric mixer set on medium speed, beat the butter for 2 minutes or until creamy. Add ½ cup of the sugar and the vanilla, and continue beating. When the mixture is fluffy, add the flour in 3 batches. Add the salt and beat for 1 minute. Add the ground pecans and beat to combine. Cover and chill for several hours.

2. Form the dough into ¾-inch balls. Place them 1 inch apart on an ungreased baking sheet. Bake for 12 to 15 minutes, until the edges are golden.

3. Meanwhile, place the remaining sugar on a plate and stir in the cinnamon.

4. While the cookies are still hot, gently roll them in the cinnamon-sugar mixture. Set aside to cool, then roll them again in the sugar, shaking off the excess.

WHILE THEY'RE STILL HOT

ROLL IN CINNAMON SUGAR

Ole! Mexican Bread Pudding

Nuts, raisins, and apples make this an extraordinary bread pudding. It's also a great way to use up day-old bread.

Butter for greasing the baking dish
1 loaf slightly stale French bread
1 cup pecans
2 cups firmly packed brown sugar
1 (2-inch) piece of cinnamon stick
2 whole cloves
4 tablespoons (½ stick) butter
4 cups water
2 large apples
1 cup raisins

1. Preheat the oven to 350°F. Lightly butter a large baking dish.

2. Cut the French bread into ¾-inch cubes. Coarsely chop the pecans. Spread out the bread cubes and chopped pecans in a single layer on a large baking sheet. Toast in the oven for 8 minutes; set aside.

3. In a medium saucepan, combine the sugar, cinnamon, cloves, butter, and water, and bring to a boil. Reduce the heat and simmer until the mixture is syrupy, about 10 to 15 minutes. Remove from the heat and set aside.

4. Peel, core, and slice the apples. In the prepared baking dish, toss the bread cubes, pecans, raisins, and apple slices.

5. Position a strainer over a medium mixing bowl. Pour the syrup through the strainer into the bowl. Discard the solids. Stir the syrup into the bread mixture.

6. Bake the pudding until golden on top, about 25 minutes. Remove from the oven and allow to cool slightly before serving.

Cinco de Mayo **135**

Best Ever Biscochitos

In New Mexico, these aniseed cookies are at every social event at Christmastime. They're equally good five months later, on Cinco de Mayo. In a tightly sealed container, they will keep for three weeks.

2 cups (4 sticks)
  unsalted butter, at
  room temperature
1 cup sugar
2 eggs
2 tablespoons aniseeds
6 cups all-purpose flour
  plus extra for the
  work surface
3 teaspoons baking
  powder
1/2 teaspoon salt
1 2/3 cup orange juice

For the topping:
1 teaspoon ground
  cinnamon
1/4 cup sugar

1. In a large mixing bowl, with an electric mixer set on medium speed, beat the butter and sugar for 3 minutes, until light and fluffy. Beat in the eggs and aniseeds.

2. Into a large bowl, sift the flour, baking powder, and salt. Add the flour mixture to the butter mixture and beat well. Add the orange juice and beat briefly. Divide the dough into 4 balls, wrap each ball in plastic, and chill for 30 minutes.

3. Preheat the oven to 350°F. Roll the dough into small balls, using your hands. Place the cookies on ungreased baking sheets. Bake until golden, about 10 to 12 minutes, depending upon how small the cookies are.

4. *Make the topping:* In a small bowl, stir the cinnamon and sugar until blended.

5. Remove the cookies from the oven and cool on the baking sheets for 4 minutes. Remove from the sheets, roll in the cinnamon mixture, and let them finish cooling on a rack.

136   *The Kids' Holiday Baking Book*

Ramadan

During the month of Ramadan, more than a billion Muslims all around the world pray and fast. Ramadan doesn't always fall at the same time of year because the Islamic calendar is a lunar calendar, meaning that it's based on the moon. Since it is about eleven days shorter than a typical year, the dates of events on the Islamic calendar move forward eleven days each year. Although the time varies on our calendar, Ramadan keeps going forward and can be at any time of year.

Muslims believe that Ramadan is the month during which Allah (God) first told a caravan trader named Muhammad about the Koran, the holy book of Islam. Each night during the month of Ramadan, Muslims recite a little of the Koran. By the end of Ramadan, they will have recited the entire Koran. Muslims call these evening prayers "tarawih."

Although children don't fast for Ramadan, grown-ups don't eat or drink anything from dawn until sunset. Hard as it might seem to go without food for so many hours, Muslims don't look at fasting as a negative experience but as a gift. The whole month is a joyous one, for Ramadan is a period when people focus on inner peace and try not to complain.

Ramadan also is a time to be hospitable and charitable to others, and Muslims take their obligation to feed hungry people seriously. At the end of each day, they break their fast with *iftar*. At this time, they may eat soups and other savory dishes. Muslims come from nearly every place in the world, so the meals they eat depend upon where they live. After the main course, Muslims move on to dessert!

The most important Muslim festival is Eid ul Fitr, the Festival of

Breaking the Fast. It's a three-day feast during which people get dressed up, decorate their homes, and visit friends and family. This is also a time to give money to the poor. Children receive gifts, money, and sweets. Here are some of the sweets you might be served at Eid ul Fitr.

Sweet Hazelnut Baklava

MAKES ABOUT
30 PIECES

Phyllo is a paper-thin dough that you can find in the freezer case at the supermarket. It makes wonderful pastries and is fairly easy to handle. Be sure to thaw it in the refrigerator overnight and keep the rolled-up sheets covered with a damp towel as you work so they won't dry out. This dessert is sweet enough for the sweetest sweet tooth!

Butter for greasing the
   baking pan

For the pastry:
1 pound hazelnuts
¼ cup sugar
1 pound frozen phyllo
   dough, thawed
½ pound (2 sticks)
   unsalted butter,
   melted

For the syrup:
1¾ cups sugar
1½ cups water
1 teaspoon lemon juice

1. Preheat the oven to 350°F. Lightly grease a 9 by 13-inch baking pan with butter.

2. *Make the pastry:* In a food processor, grind the hazelnuts with the sugar. Don't reduce it to a powder, though. The mixture should be coarse!

3. Open the package of phyllo dough and unfold it. Keep it under a damp towel. Place one half of 1 sheet in the baking pan. Let the other half extend over the side of the pan. Using a pastry brush, brush the pastry in the pan with the melted butter. Fold the other half over and brush with butter. Keep layering the phyllo sheets and brushing them with butter until you have used up about one third of the package. Sprinkle the nuts over the pastry, then layer on the remaining phyllo sheets. Be sure to brush each with melted butter. Brush the top with the remaining butter.

4. Push down on the top firmly with your hands. With a sharp knife, cut the pastry into 30 diamond-shaped pieces. Bake for about 20 minutes. Reduce the oven temperature to 300°F and bake for another 20–25 minutes, till golden.

5. *Make the syrup:* While the baklava are baking, combine the sugar and water in a medium saucepan and bring to a boil, stirring occasionally. Reduce the heat and simmer for 5 minutes. Stir in the lemon juice and simmer another 3 minutes. Remove from the heat and set aside to cool.

6. When you remove the baklava from the oven, carefully pour off any excess butter. Pour the syrup over the baklava and allow to cool in the pan for several hours. Remove to a platter and serve.

Fabulous Fig Layer Cake

SERVES 8–10

This is a very moist layer cake. If you prefer frosting on your cake, omit the fig filling and topping and frost it with White Icing (see page 87) instead.

Nonstick vegetable oil spray

For the cake:
2 cups all-purpose flour
2 teaspoons baking powder
½ teaspoon salt
¼ cup (½ stick) unsalted butter, at room temperature
1 cup granulated sugar
1 egg
1 cup evaporated milk
1 teaspoon vanilla extract
¼ teaspoon almond extract
2 teaspoons grated orange rind
1 cup chopped fresh figs

For the filling:
2 cups chopped fresh figs
¼ cup firmly packed brown sugar
¼ cup water
1 tablespoon lemon juice

1. Preheat the oven to 350°F. Lightly coat two 8-inch round cake pans with vegetable oil spray.

2. Into a medium bowl, sift the flour, baking powder, and salt; set aside.

3. In a large mixing bowl, with an electric mixer set on medium speed, cream the butter with the granulated sugar for 2 minutes, until fluffy. Add the egg and beat 1 minute. Add the flour mixture alternately with the evaporated milk, beating just until incorporated after each addition. Beat in the extracts and the grated orange rind. Stir in 1 cup of the chopped figs.

4. Divide the batter evenly between the prepared pans. Bake for 30 minutes, or until a toothpick inserted into the center comes out dry. Cool the cakes in the pans for 10 minutes. Remove to a rack and allow to cool completely.

5. *Make the filling*: In a saucepan, combine 2 cups figs, brown sugar, water, and lemon juice and bring to a boil. Reduce the heat to a simmer and cook over low heat until thickened, about 20 minutes.

6. Allow filling mixture to cool slightly. Spread a thin coating between the cake layers and on top of the cake.

Rich Semolina Cookies

MAKES 24–30 COOKIES

This became my thirteen-year-old daughter's cookie of choice when I first tested the recipe for this book.

½ cup cake flour
½ cup all-purpose flour
1 cup semolina flour
1 cup (2 sticks) unsalted butter, at room temperature
⅔ cup confectioners' sugar
¾ teaspoon orange flower water
30 blanched almonds

1. Preheat the oven to 275°F.

2. Into a medium mixing bowl, sift the cake flour, all-purpose flour, and semolina flour; set aside.

3. In a large bowl, with an electric mixer set on medium speed, beat the butter for 10 minutes, until fluffy. Add the confectioners' sugar and the orange flower water. Fold in the flour mixture gradually. Cover the dough and refrigerate it for 10 to 15 minutes.

4. Drop the dough by teaspoonfuls ½ inch apart onto ungreased baking sheets. Place an almond in the center of each cookie.

5. Bake for 20 to 30 minutes, or until golden. Do not overbake. Use a spatula to transfer the cookies to a rack. Allow them to cool for at least 1 hour.

Fig and Date Bread

MAKES 1 LOAF
(ABOUT 12 SERVINGS)

Top a slice of this sweet, dark loaf with a little cream cheese—and some extra chopped dates, if you like them.

Butter for greasing the
baking pan
1 cup chopped pitted
dates
1 cup chopped dried figs
¼ cup (½ stick)
unsalted butter,
softened
1½ teaspoons baking
soda
1 cup boiling water
½ cup sugar
½ cup chopped walnuts
2 eggs
¾ cup all-purpose flour
¾ cup whole-wheat
flour
½ teaspoon baking
powder
½ teaspoon salt

1. Preheat the oven to 350°F. Lightly grease an 8 by 4-inch loaf pan.

2. In a medium mixing bowl, combine the dates, figs, butter, and baking soda. Pour in the boiling water and stir to combine. Let stand for 15 minutes.

3. Beat the sugar, walnuts, and eggs into the date mixture.

4. Into a medium mixing bowl, sift the all-purpose flour, whole-wheat flour, baking powder, and salt. Stir the flour mixture into the date mixture just until blended.

5. Pour and scrape the batter into the prepared pan. Bake for 50 to 60 minutes or until a toothpick inserted into center of the loaf comes out clean. Cool the loaf in the pan for 10 minutes. Turn out on a wire rack to cool completely.

Stuffed Lebanese Pancakes

SERVES 8

(Atayif Mihshi)

This recipe is from Karima Maloley of the Al-Noor School in Brooklyn, who says Muslims like to eat this as a sweet after the main meal. Karima is Moroccan, and her husband is Lebanese. "When we got married, I needed to learn to cook Lebanese dishes so I bought a Lebanese cookbook," she recalls. These pancakes may be served hot or cold. A grown-up should definitely be in charge of the frying, but kids can help by sprinkling the pancakes with the nut and sugar mixture.

For the pancakes:
1 package (2¼
   teaspoons) active dry
   yeast
1¼ cups lukewarm
   water
1 teaspoon sugar
1½ cups all-purpose
   flour
Olive or nut oil for
   frying

1. *Make the pancakes:* In a small bowl, stir together the yeast, ¼ cup water, and sugar. Set in a warm place until the mixture begins to bubble, about ½ hour.

2. Into a large mixing bowl, sift the flour. Make a well in the center. Pour in the yeast mixture and rub it into the flour. Pour the remaining 1 cup lukewarm water into the flour and stir until a smooth batter forms. Cover with a towel and set it in a warm place for 1 hour, until the batter rises and is bubbly.

3. Grease the inside of a heavy frying pan with oil. Heat over medium heat until very hot but not smoking. Turn down the heat and drop a few tablespoons of batter into the pan. Tilt the pan from side to side to help the batter spread evenly. Make sure the pancake is round and fairly thick. When it begins to bubble and comes away evenly from the pan, remove to a plate. Repeat with the remaining batter, stacking the cooked pancakes on the plate.

For the filling:
- **2 cups finely chopped walnuts**
- **3 tablespoons sugar**
- **2 teaspoons ground cinnamon**
- **3 cups cold Atter syrup (see below)**

4. *Make the filling:* In a medium bowl, mix the walnuts, sugar and cinnamon. Cover the uncooked side of each pancake with the walnut-sugar mixture. Fold into half-circles and pinch the edges to secure.

5. Into a heavy frying pan, pour enough oil to reach a depth of about 1 inch. Heat over medium heat until hot. Fry the stuffed pancakes for 2 to 3 minutes, a few at a time, until golden. Drain well on paper towels. While still hot, dip in the cold Atter syrup.

Atter

(Sugar Syrup)

This syrup will keep for a few weeks when stored in the refrigerator in an airtight container. Keep it chilled so that when you pour it over the hot pancakes it will penetrate them.

3 cups sugar
1½ cups water
1 tablespoon lemon
   juice
1 teaspoon rose water

1. In a heavy saucepan, heat the sugar and water over medium heat, stirring to dissolve the sugar. Add the lemon juice and bring to a boil.

2. Skim any foam from the surface and continue to boil, stirring occasionally, for about 10 minutes or until the syrup thickens. Add the rose water and stir to combine. Let cool.

M'hal'labeeyeh

(Ground Rice Pudding)

This is also from Karima Maloley of the Al-Noor School. Rice flour can be found in specialty food stores or by mail order from Kalustyan, a specialty food store, at www.kalustyan.com. You can replace the rosewater with 1½ teaspoons of almond extract. Use whole milk for the best taste.

2 tablespoons cornstarch
¼ cup rice flour
I quart milk
I cup sugar
I teaspoon rose water
¼ cup blanched slivered almonds

1. In a small bowl, combine the cornstarch and rice flour. Stir in a little milk to form a smooth paste; set aside.

2. In a heavy, nonstick saucepan, mix the remaining milk with the sugar and bring it to a boil. Pour 3 tablespoons of the hot milk into the cornstarch paste; stir well. Lower the heat under the milk-sugar mixture to a simmer. With a wooden spoon, gradually stir the warm paste into the milk. Be careful not to scrape the bottom of the pot with your spoon. This might cause you to dislodge any particles of burned milk! Keep stirring and cooking the mixture until it is thick enough to coat the back of a spoon. Stir for 1 more minute.

3. Remove the pan from the heat and stir in the rose water. This entire stirring process should take 6–10 minutes. Cool slightly. Pour into individual dessert dishes, cover each with plastic wrap, and refrigerate.

4. When chilled, decorate with the almonds.

Independence Day and Bastille Day

As if summer isn't wonderful enough without a holiday in the middle, along comes Independence Day, with everything a patriotic celebration should have: parades, picnics, fireworks, and big family barbecues.

On this day, we commemorate the anniversary of the signing of the Declaration of Independence in 1776, when the Continental Congress declared the United States of America independent of Great Britain. Thomas Jefferson, in the preamble to the Declaration, wrote that "all men are created equal" and that they have a right to "life, liberty and the pursuit of happiness." These are beliefs that we carry in our hearts and that our laws are based on. The Declaration of Independence makes us proud to be Americans.

The Fourth of July is the perfect day to show your patriotism. Hang an American flag outside your door; wear red, white, and blue; and whip up some extra-special sweets. Of course, the best dessert on the Fourth of July is watermelon, closely followed by ice cream. But if you're in a colorful mood, the possibilities are nearly endless. Thanks to the strawberries and blueberries that start showing up in markets in the summer, you can make naturally colored red, white, and blue cookies, cakes, and pies.

Another summer holiday that comes just ten days after Independence Day is a French one called Bastille Day, whose theme also is democracy. It commemorates a day in 1789 when the citizens of Paris captured and practically destroyed a large state prison known as the Bastille. Though not many prisoners lived there, the Bastille symbolized the cruel French monarchy. Under the French king, the rich lived a luxurious life and didn't pay any taxes while the poor not only were coerced into paying heavy taxes, but also were left starving. Anyone who spoke out against these injustices was thrown into prison. The fall of the Bastille marked the beginning of the French Revolution, which overthrew the whole monarchy and was instrumental in establishing a democratic government.

Today Bastille Day is celebrated in many parts of the world with parades, dancing, music, and feasts. One of the most delicious ways to observe Bastille Day is to eat a special dessert called "crêpes." These are actually thin pancakes that you can fill with assorted fruits and top with whipped cream. You can also just spread crêpes with jam and peanut butter, roll them up, and eat them with your hands. Crêpes are easy and fun to make, too. You will need a nonstick pan to keep the crêpes from sticking. Once you've got a stack of crêpes, the only limit on how to eat them is your own wonderful imagination.

Grandma's No-Bake Lemon Icebox Dessert

My mother called this cool, citrusy pudding simply "Lemon Dessert." Make it the night before your Fourth of July barbecue, and when it's time for dessert, spoon it into dishes and top each serving with whipped cream—and a tiny flag, if you like!

55 vanilla wafers (such as Nilla wafers)
1 small package lemon Jell-O
1½ cups boiling water
Juice and grated rind of 1 lemon
½ cup sugar
½ (14-ounce) can evaporated milk, well chilled

1. Put the vanilla wafers into a resealable plastic bag, seal the bag, and pound the wafers until they are crumbs. (Alternatively, an adult can put the wafers into a food processor and pulse until they are crumbs.) Place half the crumbs in the bottom of a 9-inch pie pan.

2. In a medium mixing bowl, combine the Jell-O, boiling water, lemon juice, lemon rind, and sugar. Stir until the sugar and Jell-O have dissolved. Cover and refrigerate for about 4 hours or until the mixture has set.

3. With a handheld electric mixer set on high speed, whip the Jell-O mixture until frothy. Wash the beaters. Pour the evaporated milk into another bowl. With the electric mixer on high speed, beat the milk until frothy. With a spoon, fold it into the lemon mixture and mix well.

4. Spoon the lemon mixture into the pie pan. Sprinkle with the remaining crumbs. Cover with plastic wrap. Refrigerate for at least 4 hours or overnight.

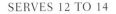

Patriotic Pound Cake with Three Berries

SERVES 12 TO 14

This is a generously proportioned party cake. Make the berry topping in the morning so it has plenty of time to chill. For a picnic, pack the topping in one container and the berries in another. Assemble the cake just before serving.

For the blueberry topping:
3 cups fresh blueberries
3 teaspoons cornstarch
9 tablespoons sugar
2 tablespoons plus 1 teaspoon water

For the cake:
Butter and flour for coating the pan
2½ cups all-purpose flour
2 teaspoons baking powder
½ teaspoon salt
1 cup (2 sticks) unsalted butter, at room temperature

1. *Make the blueberry topping:* In a 2-quart saucepan, combine the blueberries, cornstarch, sugar, and water and bring to a boil over medium heat, stirring. Cook 2 to 3 minutes, until the mixture thickens and the berries start to pop. Cool and refrigerate until serving time.

2. *Make the cake:* Preheat the oven to 325°F. Lightly grease with butter and flour a large Bundt or tube pan. (It should be large enough to hold 10 to 12 cups.)

3. In a large mixing bowl, sift the flour, baking powder, and salt; set aside.

4. With a handheld electric mixer set on medium speed, cream the butter for about 3 minutes, until very pale. Add the sugar and beat 2 minutes or until fluffy. Add the eggs, one at a time, beating well before adding the next. Add the vanilla, almond, and coconut extracts. Add the sour cream and beat 1 minute. Add the flour mixture and beat on low speed for about 30 seconds. Do not overbeat. Turn off the beater and stir the batter with a large spoon until it is blended and smooth.

2½ **cups sugar**

5 **eggs, at room temperature**

1 **teaspoon vanilla extract**

1 **teaspoon almond extract**

½ **teaspoon coconut extract**

1 **cup sour cream**

For finishing the cake:

1 **cup fresh raspberries**

1 **cup fresh strawberries, stemmed and halved**

5. Spoon the batter into the prepared pan. Bake for 1 hour to 1 hour and 15 minutes. (Start checking on it after 55 minutes). When the cake is done, a toothpick inserted in the center should come out clean.

6. Cool the cake in the pan for 15 minutes. Run a knife around the edges of the pan. Invert the cake onto a serving platter.

7. When ready to serve, spoon the chilled blueberry mixture over the cake. Arrange the raspberries and strawberries on top of the blueberry mixture. Slice and serve immediately.

Best Ever Blueberry Cake

SERVES 8

We like this homey cake so much that we freeze blueberries in the summer just to have a ready supply for when we want a taste of this in the winter. It's best in July, when fresh blueberries are at their peak. This makes a great picnic cake as well as a fine breakfast or snack.

Butter for greasing the pan
1 pint blueberries
2¼ cups all-purpose flour
½ cup sugar
¾ cup (1½ sticks) butter, chilled
1 teaspoon baking soda
1 egg
½ cup plain yogurt
1 teaspoon lemon juice

1. Preheat the oven to 400°F. Lightly butter a 9-inch springform pan.

2. Pour the berries into a strainer; wash and drain them. Place the berries in a bowl and set aside.

3. In a medium mixing bowl, stir 2 cups of the flour and the sugar. Cut the butter into small pieces and add it to the flour mixture. Rub the butter into the flour mixture with your fingers until it looks like coarse meal.

4. In a small mixing bowl, stir the remaining ¼ cup flour and the baking soda. Set aside 1½ cups of the flour-butter mixture for the topping. Combine the remaining flour-butter mixture with the flour–baking soda mixture. This is for the batter.

5. In another bowl, lightly beat the egg with a fork. Add the yogurt and the lemon juice and stir vigorously. Add this to the batter and stir with a spoon just until it is blended. Stir in 1 cup of the blueberries, being careful not to mash them.

6. Spread the batter evenly in the prepared pan. Scatter the rest of the blueberries on top. Sprinkle on the topping. Place the springform pan on a baking sheet so it won't leak onto the oven and bake for about 35 to 45 minutes. Check for doneness by pressing down on the top of the cake with your finger. If it springs back, it's done. If it is still gooey in the middle, return it to the oven for another 10 minutes and then check it again.

7. When the cake is done, remove it from the oven and cool 5 minutes. Remove the springform part of the pan. Cut the cake into wedges and serve.

Berry Lover's Classic Strawberry Shortcake

This dessert is so good that once a summer, we make an entire meal out of it. It's always memorable. I rationalize skipping the main course by telling myself that this has a lot of nutritional benefits: fiber and vitamins in the strawberries and calcium in the cream. This old-fashioned dessert is also beautiful to look at, with its sugared strawberries piled on tender biscuit halves, all decorated with clouds of whipped cream.

For the biscuits:
2 cups all-purpose flour
2 teaspoons baking powder
½ teaspoon baking soda
½ teaspoon salt
1 tablespoon granulated sugar
½ cup vegetable shortening
⅔ cup buttermilk
Flour for the work surface

For the strawberries:
2 pints strawberries
¼ cup granulated sugar

1. Preheat the oven to 425°F.

2. Into a large mixing bowl, sift the flour, baking powder, baking soda, salt, and granulated sugar. Add the shortening. With your fingertips, rub the shortening into the flour mixture until the mixture resembles coarse crumbs. Add the buttermilk and stir with a wooden spoon to form a soft dough.

3. Once it's sticking together, turn out the dough onto a lightly floured work surface. Knead it with the heel of your hand about a dozen times. Pat it out into an 8 by 8-inch square that is about ½ inch thick.

4. Using a round 2½-inch cookie cutter or the rim of an inverted drinking glass, cut out biscuits. Place them on an ungreased baking sheet. It's okay if the biscuits are touching each other because this means they will be softer. Reroll the scraps and cut out more biscuits. Bake for 15 minutes or until golden. Remove the biscuits from the oven and cool on a rack.

For the whipped cream:

2 cups heavy cream, well chilled

6 tablespoons confectioners' sugar

1 teaspoon vanilla extract

5. *Prepare the berries:* Wash the strawberries thoroughly; remove the hulls. Reserve 6 to 8 large, perfect-looking berries for garnish. Cut up the remaining berries and place them in a large bowl. Stir in the granulated sugar, cover with plastic wrap, and refrigerate for at least 15 minutes.

6. *Prepare the whipped cream:* In a medium bowl, with an electric mixer set on high speed, beat the heavy cream until soft peaks form. Add the confectioners' sugar and the vanilla extract and beat until stiff peaks form. Don't overbeat or you will have butter!

7. *Assemble the dessert:* Split 1 or 2 biscuits, depending on how hungry you are, and place in a bowl. Spoon some strawberries in between and on top of the halves. Top with a generous serving of whipped cream and place 1 whole berry in the center of the top, for garnish. Repeat with the remaining biscuits, strawberries, and whipped cream until everyone has been served.

Independence Day and Bastille Day **157**

Chocolate-Chip Blondies

MAKES 16

My mother-in-law makes these buttery squares each year and serves them at her Fourth-of-July barbecues. It's very hard to eat just one.

Cooking spray or butter
  for greasing the pan
2 eggs
1½ cups all-purpose
  flour
1½ teaspoons baking
  powder
½ teaspoon salt
1 cup sugar
⅓ cup vegetable oil
2 cups mini chocolate
  chips

1. Preheat the oven to 350°F. Lightly grease an 8-inch square baking pan with cooking spray or butter.

2. In a small bowl, beat the eggs with a fork and set aside. Into a large mixing bowl, sift the flour, baking powder, salt, and sugar.

3. Add the oil to the flour mixture and beat with an electric mixer set on medium speed for 1 minute. Add the beaten eggs and beat for 1 minute or until the batter is thoroughly blended. Stir in the chocolate chips.

4. Spoon the batter into the prepared pan and spread it around evenly. It will be very stiff. Bake for 25 to 30 minutes, just until the top is golden brown. Remove from the oven and cool for 20 minutes on a rack. Cut into squares.

Lemon Flag Bars

These rich bars have a shortbread crust and a topping that's red (frosting), white (confectioners' sugar), and blue (berries).

For the crust:
Butter for greasing the
   pan
½ cup (1 stick) butter,
   at room temperature
½ cup firmly packed
   light brown sugar
1½ cups all-purpose
   flour
1 teaspoon grated
   lemon rind

For the lemon filling:
1½ cups granulated
   sugar
½ cup freshly squeezed
   lemon juice
½ cup water
2 tablespoons cornstarch
2 eggs
2 teaspoons grated
   lemon rind

1. Preheat the oven to 350°F. Grease a 9-inch square baking pan.

2. *Make the crust*: In a large mixing bowl, with an electric mixer set on medium speed, beat the ½ cup butter and brown sugar for 2 minutes or until light and fluffy. Turn the mixer speed to low and beat in the flour and lemon zest. Pat the dough evenly into the prepared pan.

3. *Make the lemon filling*: In a heavy 2-quart saucepan, whisk 1 cup of the granulated sugar, lemon juice, water, and cornstarch. Cook over medium-high heat, stirring constantly, for several minutes. When it thickens, cook 1 minute more and then remove from the heat.

4. In a medium mixing bowl, whisk the remaining ½ cup granulated sugar, eggs, and lemon rind until thick and lemon-colored. Slowly beat the lemon mixture into the egg mixture, until well combined.

5. Pour the filling into the prepared crust. Bake for 15 or 20 minutes or until the filling is firm. Cool completely in the pan on a rack.

For the topping:
¼ cup confectioners' sugar
I tube red gel frosting
½ cup fresh blueberries

6. Cut into 6 rectangular bars. Place the bars on a pretty serving plate. Sprinkle the cookies with confectioners' sugar. Use the gel frosting to create stripes across the cookies. Arrange 6 blueberries in the top left corner of each bar.

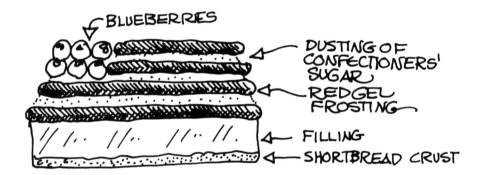

BLUEBERRIES

DUSTING OF CONFECTIONERS' SUGAR

RED GEL FROSTING

FILLING

SHORTBREAD CRUST

Bastille Day Parisian Crêpes

The French word for pancake is crêpe, *and these are pancakes extraordinaire. A special Bastille Day treat, these may be frozen for up to two months, with a single layer of waxed paper between each one. They're very versatile—besides sweet fillings, you can use meats, cheeses and vegetables, in which case you can call them dinner.*

2 tablespoons butter
2 eggs
1 cup milk
½ teaspoon salt
1 cup all-purpose flour
3 teaspoons butter for coating the pan

1. In a small saucepan, melt the butter over low heat; set aside to cool.

2. In a medium mixing bowl, beat the eggs very well with an egg beater or with an electric mixer set on low speed. Add the milk, salt, flour, and butter; beat until smooth. Cover and let stand at room temperature for about 30 minutes.

3. Heat a 7-inch nonstick skillet or crêpe pan over medium-high heat. When it is very hot, apply a very thin film of butter using a paper towel. Pour in several tablespoons of batter, then tilt the pan so that it spreads evenly, coating the bottom of the pan. Cook for about two minutes.

4. When the bottom is golden and you can easily lift the edges up from the pan, turn it over with a spatula. Cook for another 1 or 2 minutes. Remove to a plate, apply a very thin film of butter to the pan, and make more crêpes.

5. There are several ways to eat crêpes. You can simply spread one with strawberry or raspberry jam, roll it up, and eat it. Or you can slice and sugar some strawberries, roll them into a crêpe, and top with whipped cream. Or try topping a crêpe with delicious Maine Blueberry Sauce (see following recipe).

Maine Blueberry Sauce

SERVES 4

This is good with crêpes, pancakes, and as an ice cream topping.

2 pints blueberries
⅓ cup sugar
1 tablespoon instant
   tapioca
Juice of 1 lemon

1. Place the berries in a medium saucepan and sprinkle them with the sugar. Sprinkle with the tapioca and the lemon juice and stir until well combined. Set aside for 15 minutes.

2. Cook the berries over low heat for about 10 minutes, stirring constantly. When the berries soften and pop and the juice starts to thicken, the sauce is ready. Cool it slightly before serving. Store it in the refrigerator.

Rosh Hashanah

A New Year's celebration in the fall? Each year in September or October, Jewish people observe Rosh Hashanah, which commemorates the anniversary of Creation and signifies the start of a brand-new year.

Jewish people believe that on this day, God opens the Book of Life and observes his creatures, deciding their fate for the coming year. God's judgment isn't final, however, until the book is "sealed" ten days later, on Yom Kippur. The time in between, called Shabbat Shuva, is a period during which Jews reflect and think about justifying their lives to God.

Rosh Hashanah is observed on the first two days of Tishrei, the seventh month of the Jewish calendar, which typically falls anywhere from mid-September to early October. Jewish holidays are determined by the lunar calendar, not the solar one, and thus they fall on different days every year.

The words *Rosh Hashanah* come from the Hebrew words *rosh*, which means "head" or "beginning," and *hashanah*, which means "year." Jewish people call the ten-day period that starts with Rosh Hashanah and ends with Yom Kippur the Days of Awe, or simply the High Holy Days. Rosh Hashanah is the only major Jewish celebration that last for two days, and prayer is very important. The shofar, which is made from an animal's horn, preferably a ram's, is sounded a hundred times each day of Rosh Hashanah. The sound of the shofar reminds the soul to repent, and warns Jews to resist temptation.

At Rosh Hashanah, Jewish families wear special clothes and children receive treats. Although certain types of work are forbidden, cooking is thankfully not one of them. Seasonal foods that are plentiful, such as apples, pomegranates, and grapes, are eaten. Apples are dipped in honey, signifying the hopes for a sweet year ahead.

Challah, a special bread that Jewish people eat on the Sabbath and on holidays, is usually in the shape of a long braid. But on Rosh Hashanah, Jewish cooks coil the dough into a round, which symbolizes the hopes for a well-rounded and full year. The round loaf also recalls the crown of God's kingdom.

Desserts made with apples, such as cakes and crisps, are very popular on Rosh Hashanah. And Rosh Hashanah is the perfect occasion to make a moist, dense honey cake that is eaten in small pieces because it is so rich. A special cookie called "tayglach" consists of little pieces of dough that are cooked in a delicious honey glaze. You decide for yourself if it seems more like a cookie or a candy.

Happy New Year Apple Cake

SERVES 8

This is good with a big scoop of slightly softened vanilla ice cream, or you can sprinkle the top with some confectioners' sugar instead.

Margarine and flour for coating the pan

3 cooking apples (such as Rome Beauty)

2 teaspoons ground cinnamon

2⅓ cups sugar (divided)

1 cup margarine, at room temperature

4 eggs

3 cups sifted all-purpose flour

3 teaspoons baking powder

½ teaspoon salt

⅓ cup orange juice

1½ teaspoons vanilla extract

1 teaspoon almond extract

1. Preheat oven to 350°F. Lightly grease and flour a 10-inch tube pan.

2. Peel, core, and quarter the apples. Cut the quarters into thin slices. In a medium bowl, toss the apple slices, cinnamon, and ⅓ cup of the sugar.

3. In a large mixing bowl, with an electric mixer set on medium speed, beat the margarine and the remaining 2 cups sugar for 2 minutes or until fluffy. Add the eggs, one at a time, mixing well after addition.

4. Into a separate bowl, sift the flour, baking powder, and salt. Add to the batter. Beat for 30 seconds. Add the orange juice and extracts; beat until smooth.

5. Place a small amount of batter in the bottom of the prepared pan. Arrange a layer of apple slices over the batter. Continue layering, ending with batter. Bake for 1 hour and 15 minutes to 1 hour and 30 minutes, or until a cake tester inserted into the center comes out clean.

6. Cool the cake in the pan for 10 minutes. Loosen the edges with a table knife and invert onto a serving plate. Allow to finish cooling on a wire rack.

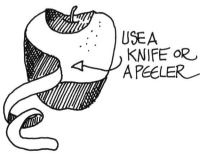

USE A KNIFE OR A PEELER

Chocolate Rocks

MAKES 2 DOZEN

These look like rocks, but don't be fooled! They are chewy, crunchy, and perfectly sweet candies. Plus they're a snap to make—you don't even have to turn on the oven.

1 (6-ounce) package semisweet chocolate chips
½ cup chopped peanuts
½ cup raisins
½ cup puffed-rice cereal
¾ cup marshmallow cream

1. In the top of a double boiler over simmering water, melt the chocolate chips. Let cool slightly.

2. In a small bowl, stir the peanuts, raisins, and puffed rice.

3. Stir the marshmallow cream into the melted chocolate. Add the nut mixture to the chocolate mixture; stir until everything is coated with chocolate. Drop by teaspoonfuls onto a sheet of parchment paper. Allow to harden and cool for about 1 hour.

Apple-Pecan Crisp

A crisp is a baked fruit dessert with a crunchy (and crisp) topping. For this one, use an apple that holds its shape and isn't too sweet. Rome Beauties, Cortlands, and Gravensteins all make flavorful apple crisp.

Margarine for greasing
  the baking pan
1 cup all-purpose flour
1½ cups firmly packed
  brown sugar
½ to 1 cup chopped
  pecans (optional)
½ cup oatmeal (quick-
  cooking)
½ cup (1 stick)
  margarine
8 to 10 apples

1. Preheat the oven to 375°F. Lightly grease a 9-inch square baking pan.

2. In a large mixing bowl, combine the flour, brown sugar, pecans, and oatmeal. Add the margarine and work it into the mixture with your fingers until crumbly.

3. Peel, core, and quarter the apples. Cut the quarters into thin slices. Sprinkle some of the sugar/flour mixture over the bottom of the prepared pan. Cover with a layer of apples. Add another layer of the sugar/flour mixture and then another layer of apples. Finish with the sugar/flour mixture. Bake for 1 hour or until the apples are soft.

Little Bear's Honey Cake

(Lekakh)

The Yiddish word for honey cake is Lekakh. It's traditionally served on Rosh Hashanah and other happy occasions, to ensure a sweet year. This cake usually calls for coffee, but I've substituted decaf coffee. You can use either brewed or instant.

Vegetable oil and flour for coating the baking pan

2 cups honey (divided)

¾ cup vegetable oil

I cup brewed decaf coffee

2½ teaspoons vanilla extract

3¾ cups all-purpose flour

I½ teaspoons baking soda

I teaspoon baking powder

2 teaspoons ground cinnamon

½ teaspoon ground nutmeg

3 eggs

¾ cup sugar

1. Preheat the oven to 350°F. Oil and flour a 13 by 9-inch baking pan.

2. In a heavy saucepan, combine 1½ cups of the honey, the oil, coffee, and vanilla and cook, stirring, over very low heat for several minutes, until thoroughly blended. Set aside to cool.

3. Into a large mixing bowl, sift the flour, baking soda, baking powder, cinnamon, and nutmeg.

4. In another large mixing bowl, with an electric mixer set on high speed, beat the eggs with the sugar for 5 minutes. Beat the cooled honey mixture into the eggs. Sift in the flour mixture and beat the batter on medium speed for 2 minutes.

5. Spoon and scrape the batter into the prepared pan. Bake for 40 minutes or until the cake springs back when pressed in the center.

6. Remove the cake from the oven and prick holes all over the top with a fork. Heat the remaining ½-cup honey in a small saucepan. Spread the honey all over the cake. Cool the cake in the pan, then cut into squares.

PRICK TOP OF THE CAKE WITH A FORK

SPREAD WITH WARM HONEY
SPREAD HONEY

THE HOLES HELP THE HONEY SINK IN

Holiday Honey Cookies

MAKES ABOUT 6 DOZEN

Called "tayglach," these sweet confections are a Rosh Hashanah specialty. Traditionally, the dough is cooked in a honey syrup on top of the stove, which is messy and time consuming. It's much easier to bake the cookies in the syrup, right in the oven. You will need small paper candy cups for these cookies, because they're rather sticky from the honey.

Nonstick cooking spray

For the cookies:
3 eggs
2 tablespoons vegetable oil
1 tablespoon grated orange rind
2 cups all-purpose flour
1 teaspoon baking powder

For the syrup and topping:
¾ cup honey
½ cup sugar
1 teaspoon ground ginger
¾ cup chopped walnuts

For decoration:
½ cup shredded coconut
¼ cup colored sprinkles

1. Line a baking sheet with parchment paper. Spray the paper with nonstick cooking spray.

2. *Make the cookies:* Preheat the oven to 375°F. In a large mixing bowl, with an electric mixer set on medium speed, beat the eggs, oil, and orange rind for 1 minute or until well blended. Add the flour and the baking powder and mix well. Use your hands to shape the mixture into seven (2-inch) balls. Roll each ball into a 10-inch-long rope. Cut each rope into half-inch pieces.

3. *Make the syrup:* In a large, heavy, ovenproof saucepan, stir the honey, sugar, and ginger and bring to a boil. Add the cookies and stir until they are well coated. Remove from the heat.

4. Place the pan in the oven and bake, covered with foil, for 18 to 20 minutes. Add the walnuts and stir well, being sure to separate the pieces of dough. Bake, covered, for 10 to 20 minutes more, stirring after every 10 minutes.

5. When the cookies are browned and crisp, remove them from the oven. Pour and scrape the browned cookies and syrup onto the prepared baking sheet. Spread out in a single layer.

6. *Toast the coconut*: Reduce the oven temperature to 350°F. Place the coconut on an ungreased baking sheet. Bake for 8 to 10 minutes, stirring occasionally, until golden. Sprinkle the cookies with the coconut and the sprinkles. Let cool completely, then form the cookies into little mounds of about 5 cookies each. Place each little mound in a paper candy cup.

Poppyseed-Topped Challah

MAKES 2 LOAVES

Challah may not seem like a dessert per se, but it's so traditional at Rosh Hashanah (and at many Jewish celebrations) that I have decided to include a recipe. It is, after all, sweet! When you want something that's delicious, wholesome, and not too sugary, challah is perfect.

Margarine for greasing large bowl and the baking sheets
6½ to 7½ cups all-purpose flour
2 tablespoons sugar
2 teaspoons salt
2 packages active dry yeast
2 cups water
¼ cup (½ stick) butter
3 eggs, at room temperature
Flour for the work surface
1 egg yolk
1 tablespoon cold water
1 teaspoon poppy seeds

1. Lightly grease a very large bowl; set aside.

2. In another large mixing bowl, stir 2 cups of the flour, the sugar, salt, and yeast; set aside.

3. In a medium heavy saucepan, heat the 2 cups of water with the butter over low heat, until the mixture is very warm. It should not be so hot that you can't hold your hand in it. If you have a kitchen thermometer, check the temperature of the mixture. It should be between 120° and 130°F. It's okay if the butter has not completely melted.

4. Pour the liquid mixture into the flour mixture and beat with an electric mixer set on low speed for 30 seconds or just until mixed. Turn the beater to medium speed and beat, scraping bowl occasionally with a rubber spatula, for 2 minutes.

5. Beat in the eggs and 1½ cups of the flour. Keep beating, occasionally scraping the bowl, for 2 minutes or until you have a thick batter.

6. Stir in more flour (about 3 cups). You should have a soft dough. If not, add a bit more flour and stir. Turn out the dough onto a lightly floured work surface.

KNEAD DOUGH

Knead the dough until smooth and elastic, about 10 minutes, gradually adding more flour if needed.

7. Shape the dough into a ball. Place it in the large greased bowl and turn the dough over to grease the top. Cover with a towel and let rise in a warm place for 1 hour or until doubled in bulk.

8. Punch down the dough and push the edges of the dough into the center of the bowl. Place the dough on a lightly floured work surface. Cut it in half, cover, and let rest for 15 minutes.

PUNCH DOWN THE DOUGH

9. Lightly grease 2 large baking sheets. With your hands, roll half the dough into a 32-inch-long smooth rope. Beginning with one end, wind it into a 5-inch circle, spiraling it up in a coil like a snail. Tuck the remaining end underneath. Repeat with the remaining dough to make a second loaf.

COIL THE DOUGH

10. Transfer the round loaves to the greased baking sheets. Cover the loaves with a towel and let rise in a warm place until doubled in bulk, about 1 hour.

11. Preheat the oven to 400°F. In a small bowl, beat the egg yolk with the tablespoon of cold water. Brush the loaves with the glaze. Sprinkle them with poppy seeds.

12. Bake for 25 minutes or until the tops are golden and the loaves sound hollow when you tap one with your finger. Remove from the baking sheets to a wire rack and allow to cool completely.

Apple Noodle Kugel

SERVES 6

It's a tradition to serve a kugel, which is basically a baked pudding, as a side dish on the sabbath. When it is made with sweet ingredients, like sugar and spices, it can be a dessert. This is a not-too-sweet pudding that is good for a meal or a dessert.

Margarine for greasing the baking pan
½ pound egg noodles
3 apples
4 eggs
¾ cup cold water
3 tablespoons freshly squeezed lemon juice
¼ teaspoon kosher salt
1¼ cups sugar
1 teaspoon vanilla extract
½ cup raisins
¼ cup orange juice

For the topping:
2 tablespoons sugar
1 teaspoon ground cinnamon
¼ teaspoon ground nutmeg
2 tablespoons margarine

1. Preheat the oven to 350°F. Lightly grease a 2-quart baking dish.

2. Cook the noodles according to the package directions. Drain and set aside.

3. Peel and core the apples. Quarter them and cut them into slices.

4. In a small bowl, lightly beat the eggs with a whisk.

5. In a large bowl, combine the noodles, apples, water, lemon juice, salt, 1¼ cups of sugar, vanilla, raisins, orange juice, and beaten eggs; stir until thoroughly mixed. Spoon and scrape into the prepared baking dish.

6. *Make the topping:* In a small bowl, stir the 2 tablespoons of sugar, cinnamon, and nutmeg. Sprinkle over the pudding. Dot with the margarine. Bake for 45 minutes to 1 hour, until thoroughly hot and crisp on top. Serve the pudding warm. Be sure to refrigerate leftovers.

SERVE WARM

Raisin-Farfel Kugel

SERVES 6

A kugel is usually made with potatoes or some type of noodle. This one contains farfel pasta, which is also called "egg-barley" pasta. It starts as a dough that is formed into little barley-size lumps. It can be boiled, fried, or baked, and it is often served with roast meats. But after tasting this, you will agree that farfel pasta tastes best as dessert!

Butter or margarine for
  greasing the baking
  pan
2 cups farfel pasta
6 eggs
½ cup raisins
½ teaspoon salt
1 cup sugar
1 tablespoon ground
  cinnamon
4 tablespoons (½ stick)
  butter or margarine,
  at room temperature

1. Preheat the oven to 350°F. Lightly grease an 8-inch square baking dish.

2. In a medium bowl, soak the farfel in water to cover for 10 minutes; drain.

3. Beat the eggs vigorously with a whisk. Add the beaten eggs to the bowl of farfel. Let stand for 10 minutes.

4. Stir in the raisins, salt, sugar, cinnamon, and butter. Transfer the mixture to the prepared dish. Bake for 50 to 60 minutes, until thoroughly hot and nice and crusty on top. Serve warm.

Halloween

Can you recall your earliest memory of Halloween? Chances are good that it has to do with candy! But thousands of years ago, when this ancient celebration first got started, it was a dark, somber occasion that had nothing to do with sweets.

Halloween first began in the area of Europe that is now northern France, England, Scotland, Wales, and Ireland, which was then populated by the Celtic people, who hunted and herded to support their families. The priests of the Celts, called Druids, began their new year on what is now November 1. They believed that this date marked the start of winter, and that winter and summer were at war. On the eve of the new year, they thought, winter's army, made up of ghosts, witches, goblins, and so forth, would arrive. In order to frighten away these evil creatures, people built bonfires and wore masks and animal skins. The festival, called "Samhain" on the Celtic seasonal calendar, gave the Celts a link to their ancestors and to the past. It was marked by witchcraft and the start of a season that belonged to evil spirits.

Gradually, as Christianity spread across Europe, the Church looked for a way to replace the festival of Samhain, and the occasion was gradually assimilated into two other feasts: All Saints and All Souls. November 1 became All Saint's Day, and the night before it was called All Hallow's Eve, or Halloween.

Here in the United States, after the American Revolution, Halloween became a community celebration every fall that was a cross between a harvest get-together and a party. There was cornhusking and apple paring, plus some entertainment and dancing to keep the mood lighthearted. Another favorite pastime was storytelling, and ghost tales were always popular.

The scary animal skins and masks had long since been retired and costumes took their place. Dressed up as ghosts, goblins, black cats, and skeletons, kids began going out asking for treats and saying they'd play a trick if the candies weren't forthcoming.

Candy was the primary reason we loved Halloween as kids, but we had to eat our fill of it before we went to bed that night because the next day, it would be taken away from us. My sisters and I would come home from trick-or-treating, take off our costumes, and haul our bulging, sweet-filled sacks to the third floor, where we shared a couple of large bedrooms. There, we'd stuff ourselves silly. Sometimes I ate so much chocolate that I had to eat a Payday or two in between, just to counteract the sweet milk-chocolaty taste with a somewhat salty food. The day after Halloween, right after we came home from Mass, my mother would dump all the rest of our Halloween candy into the large metal dishpan that she used to make bread dough. Off it went to the local orphanage so the children living there would be able to have some holiday treats themselves. For us, that signaled the end of our no-holds-barred candy consumption until the next time we went trick-or-treating.

Of course, candy wasn't the only treat handed out in our neighborhood on Halloween. Each year my parents made popcorn balls that were so popular that kids who lived on nearby streets would stop by to sample them. (This was back in the days when trick-or-treaters were permitted to accept homemade goodies.) To make popcorn balls, my father concocted a sweet syrup, coated the popcorn with it, and then let us form fist-size balls of popcorn with our buttered hands.

We also made a "shortcut" caramel coating for apples by unwrapping a bag of caramels and melting them. After dipping the apples into the sweet golden syrup, we'd put a stick into each one and then roll them in chopped peanuts.

Besides apples, my favorite fall fruit has always been pumpkins. I

love how they pop up in doorways, perch as grinning jack-o'-lanterns in windows, and decorate party tables. These giant orange gourds are also the basis of Halloween desserts like pumpkin muffins and cookies.

Our Halloween is spooky and sweet all at the same time, but in Mexico, a similar holiday takes place at the very beginning of November. *El día de los muertos*, the Day of the Dead, is a holiday that is partially celebrated at night—and in cemeteries—but in a joyful manner! Families make offerings of food and drink to their deceased relatives, and during the day, they place flowers on the grave site. Altars (*ofrendas* in Spanish) are built inside homes, and families prepare special foods. On the family altar, there might be pictures of the deceased relatives, along with chocolate, bananas, tangerines, sugar skulls with names written on them, and lit candles. An important character on this day is the symbol of death, the *calavera*. This is the word for "skull," or "skeleton," in Spanish, and it's common to see figurines of skeletons doing everyday activities, like washing dishes or making tortillas or playing a musical instrument. Besides sugar skulls, the *calavera* also shows up in *pan de muerto*, a sweet bread fashioned into the shape of a skull.

Haystacks

Make these crunchy, funny-looking cookies ahead of time so they have a chance to cool. You can also place them in a plastic bag and freeze.

> 1 (6-ounce) package
> butterscotch morsels
> 1 (5-ounce) can chow
> mein noodles
> ¾ cup peanuts

1. In a medium mixing bowl, heat the butterscotch morsels in the microwave oven on Low for 2 minutes, until melted. Heat again for 30 seconds if needed. Remove from the microwave and stir.

2. Add the chow mein noodles and the peanuts and mix well.

3. Drop by teaspoonfuls onto a sheet of waxed paper and let cool for 1 hour. Peel from the paper and store in an airtight container.

Witches' Brew

This warm punch looks extra-spooky when served in a black pot. Stick three small oranges with eight whole cloves each and place the oranges in the brew. If you prefer a cold drink, this is also excellent when chilled.

1½ cups canned
   unsweetened
   pineapple juice
1 quart apple juice
3 tablespoons honey
2 tablespoons fresh
   lemon juice
3 cinnamon sticks

1. In a medium saucepan, combine all the ingredients. Warm over low heat, stirring occasionally, for about 15 minutes.

2. Remove the cinnamon sticks. Ladle the brew into small cups and serve.

Ghoulish Orange Popcorn Balls

Store these nice party treats in little plastic bags and tie each one with a black ribbon.

6 tablespoons (¾ stick)
  butter
3 cups miniature
  marshmallows
3 tablespoons dry
  orange Jell-O
12 cups unsalted popped
  popcorn
Butter for greasing your
  hands

1. In a small saucepan, melt the 6 tablespoons of butter. Add the marshmallows and stir over low heat until they have melted.

2. Remove the pan from the heat and add the orange Jell-O. Pour the marshmallow mixture over the popcorn and stir to coat.

3. Butter your hands to keep the popcorn from sticking. Form the popcorn into balls with your hands. Let dry. Store in individual plastic bags.

Spooky Chocolate-Chip Pizza

SERVES 12 OR MORE

There's no cheese on this dessert pizza, which is fun to serve at a party. You can use M&M's or Skittles instead of chocolate chips if you like.

½ cup firmly packed brown sugar

½ cup granulated sugar

½ cup (1 stick) butter, at room temperature

½ cup peanut butter

½ teaspoon vanilla extract

1 egg

1½ cups all-purpose flour

2 cups miniature marshmallows

1 (6-ounce) bag semisweet chocolate chips

½ cup pecan halves (or you can use peanuts instead)

1. Preheat the oven to 375°F. Position an oven rack in the middle of the oven.

2. In a large mixing bowl, combine the brown sugar, granulated sugar, butter, peanut butter, vanilla, and egg. With a handheld electric mixer set on medium speed, beat until well blended. Add the flour and stir with a wooden spoon until a soft dough forms.

3. Press the dough evenly over the bottom of a 12-inch pizza pan, forming a rim along the edge with your fingers. Place the pan in the oven and bake for 10 minutes or until the pizza is golden.

4. Remove the pan from the oven and sprinkle the pizza with the marshmallows, chocolate chips, and pecans. These should be evenly distributed over the pizza. Return the pan to the oven and bake for another 3 to 5 minutes.

5. When the marshmallows are puffy and golden, remove the pan from the oven. Allow the pizza to cool. Cut into wedges and serve.

PIZZA FOR DESSERT!

MARSHMALLOS CHOCOLATE CHIPS + NUTS

Pumpkin-☆Oatmeal Cookies

MAKES 2 DOZEN

These homey cookies not only taste great, they look festive. Pumpkin and oatmeal boost their nutritional value.

Cooking spray for greasing the baking sheets
2 cups all-purpose flour
1 cup quick-cooking oats
1 teaspoon baking soda
1 teaspoon ground cinnamon
½ teaspoon salt
1 cup (2 sticks) butter, at room temperature
1 cup firmly packed brown sugar
1 cup granulated sugar
1 egg, lightly beaten
1 teaspoon vanilla extract
1 cup canned pumpkin
1 cup chocolate chips
Candy corn and raisins for decorating (optional)
½ cup Vanilla Icing (p. 235) (optional)

1. Preheat the oven to 350°F. Lightly spray some baking sheets with cooking spray.

2. In a mixing bowl, stir the flour, oats, baking soda, cinnamon, and salt.

3. In a medium mixing bowl, with a handheld electric mixer set on medium speed, cream the butter for 1 minute. Gradually add the two sugars and continue to beat until light and fluffy. Add the egg and vanilla and beat for 1 minute. Add half the flour mixture and beat 2 minutes. Add half the canned pumpkin and beat for 1 minute. Add the remaining flour mixture and remaining pumpkin and beat well. Stir in the chocolate chips.

4. For each cookie, scoop ¼ cup of dough onto the prepared baking sheet. Spread into a pumpkin shape with a spatula or your fingers. Add a bit more dough to form a stem. Bake for 15 to 20 minutes, until golden brown. With a spatula, remove the cookies to a rack to cool.

5. When the cookies are cool, decorate them with raisins or candy corn by gluing these on with a dab of icing, if desired.

A BIT OF ICING HOLDS THE DECORATIONS ONTO THE COOKIE

Mexican Pan de Muerto

MAKES 1 BIG LOAF

Pan de muerto, or "bread of the dead," is shaped like bones. Mexicans eat it on El Día de los Muertos. With a slight orange flavor, this sweet bread is good for breakfast when toasted. It's fun for kids to make because the dough is easy to handle.

½ cup (1 stick) butter
1 orange
2 packages active dry yeast
1 cup warm water
½ cup sugar
3 eggs, at room temperature, lightly beaten with a fork
¼ teaspoon ground aniseed
1 teaspoon salt
4½ to 5 cups all-purpose flour
Cooking spray for the baking sheet

For the top:
1 large egg
1 tablespoon water
1 tablespoon sugar

1. Place the butter in a small glass bowl. Heat it in the microwave on high for 1 minute or until it has melted. Set aside to cool.

2. Grate the orange rind with a fine grater. Measure ½ teaspoon of the grated rind into a small bowl. Reserve the rest for another use.

3. In a large mixing bowl, combine the yeast and the warm water and stir until the yeast has dissolved. Let it stand for about 5 minutes. The yeast should begin to bubble.

4. Stir in the cooled butter. Add the sugar, eggs, orange rind, aniseed, and salt. Add 2 cups of the flour to the mixture. With an electric mixer set on medium speed, beat the dough about 2 minutes, until smooth. Add 2 more cups of the flour, 1 cup at a time, stirring well until all the flour is moistened. Add ½ cup more flour and stir. Cover the dough with plastic wrap and refrigerate for 2 hours.

5. Sprinkle a work surface with a little of the remaining flour. Place the dough on the work surface and sprinkle with a little flour. Knead it by putting the heel of one hand on the center of the dough and pressing outward and down with your other hand. Turn the dough a little bit and knead again. Repeat for about 1 minute.

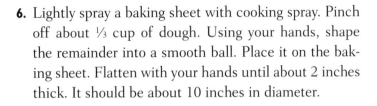

6. Lightly spray a baking sheet with cooking spray. Pinch off about ⅓ cup of dough. Using your hands, shape the remainder into a smooth ball. Place it on the baking sheet. Flatten with your hands until about 2 inches thick. It should be about 10 inches in diameter.

7. Divide the reserved ⅓ cup of dough into three equal pieces. Roll two of the pieces into two 8-inch-long ropes. Flatten the ends. In a small bowl, beat the egg with the tablespoon of water for a few seconds. Brush this egg glaze over the top of the loaf with a little brush. (A thick, clean paintbrush works well.) Carefully place the ropes over the loaf so they form an X.

8. Divide the third piece of dough into two parts. Shape one part into a ball. Paint the bottom of the ball with the egg glaze and press it into the center of the crossed ropes. Cut the remainder of the dough into four pieces and roll into teardrop shapes. Place these on the loaf, near the top, and press in firmly. Brush the top of the loaf with more of the glaze and cover it with a damp clean towel. Set it in a warm place (like the top of the stove) and let it rise until puffy, about 45 minutes.

9. Preheat the oven to 375°F. Brush the loaf again with the glaze. Sprinkle the top with 1 tablespoon sugar and bake for 30 minutes. Check for doneness by inserting a metal skewer into the center of the loaf. If it comes out clean and the loaf is nice and brown, the bread is done. If it is still sticky, return it to the oven for another 5 minutes and test it again. Remove the bread from the oven and transfer it to a wire rack to cool.

Creepy Nightcrawlers

SERVES 12

This dessert is truly creepy looking! If you've never eaten a wormy apple before, here's your chance to try one—and to give your party guests the same opportunity! A grown-up should definitely prep the apples.

12 large firm apples
¼ cup (½ stick) butter
½ cup raspberry jam
12 gummy worms

1. Preheat the oven to 350°F. With a sharp paring knife, carefully core the apples from the stem end to about ½-inch from the bottom. Don't push the knife all the way through because you don't want the filling to leak out. Carefully stuff 1 teaspoon of butter into each hole. Spoon in about a teaspoon or so of jam.

TAKE OUT THE CORE

½ INCH

2. Arrange the apples in a single layer in a large baking dish. Add about 1 inch of water. Bake them, uncovered, for 35 to 45 minutes. The baking time depends on the size of the apples. When they are done, they should be just tender but not mushy and losing their shape. Allow the apples to cool at room temperature for about 10 minutes.

3. Place the baked apples in 12 cereal or dessert bowls and carefully spoon some of the syrup from the baking pan around each. Insert a gummy worm in the top of each apple, making sure that at least half of its body is sticking out!

Dirt Pudding Pie

SERVES 12

This tastes like a creamy Oreo cheesecake—everyone loves it. As an alternative to one large pie, you can line small, clean flowerpots with aluminum foil and press cookie crumbs into the bottom and up the sides. Fill with pudding and then sprinkle tops with more cookie crumbs. Poke a gummy worm out of each flowerpot.

30 Oreo cookies

½ cup (1 stick) butter

6 ounces cream cheese, softened

2 small packages instant vanilla pudding mix (3.4 ounces each)

2½ cups milk

½ of one (12-ounce) container Cool Whip, thawed

12 gummy worms for garnish (optional)

1. Put the Oreos in a plastic bag, seal the top, and crush the cookies by pounding on them. Or ask a grown-up to crush them in a food processor.

2. In a large glass mixing bowl, heat the butter in the microwave oven on High for about 1 minute, or until it has melted. Stir in the Oreo crumbs and mix well. Reserve 1 cup of crumbs for the topping. Press the remaining crumbs into the bottom and up the sides of a deep 10-inch pie plate.

3. In the work bowl of a food processor, beat the cream cheese for 1 minute or until fluffy. Add the pudding mix and the milk and process until creamy. Spoon and scrape into a large mixing bowl. Add the Cool Whip to the cream cheese mixture and stir with a large spoon until blended.

4. Spoon and scrape the mixture into the prepared crust, mounding slightly in the center. Sprinkle with the reserved Oreo crumbs, cover, and refrigerate for several hours or until firm. Garnish with gummy worms, if desired, before serving.

DIRT PUDDING PIE

DON'T FORGET THE GUMMY WORM!

Frozen Chocolate Jack-o'-Lanterns

Make these delicious frozen treats a few hours before you plan to serve them so they have time to freeze, and try to use large seedless oranges.

6 large oranges
1 quart chocolate ice cream
6 cinnamon sticks

1. Carefully cut the tops of the oranges. Scoop out the center from each orange, leaving just a thick shell. Draw a scary or funny jack-o'-lantern face on each orange. Carefully fill the hollowed-out oranges with chocolate ice cream.

2. Using a sharp knife, carefully cut a hole large enough to insert a cinnamon stick into each orange top. Either place the tops back onto the filled oranges or leave them off, if you like. Insert a cinnamon stick through each hole, or insert directly into the ice cream. Freeze for at least 3 hours before serving.

Dracula's-Blood Milkshakes

SERVES 6

Strawberries and strawberry ice cream are the "blood" in this spooky dessert, but don't worry, it tastes just like a fruity milkshake!

3 cups vanilla yogurt
1 (10-ounce) package
   frozen strawberries
½ teaspoon vanilla
   extract
6 ice cubes
1 pint strawberry ice
   cream

1. In a blender, combine the yogurt, frozen strawberries, and vanilla extract. Whirl until smooth. Chill for at least 1 hour.

2. Place 1 ice cube in each of 6 tall glasses. Pour the blended mixture into the glasses. Top each with a small scoopful of slightly softened strawberry ice cream.

Monster Cupcakes

Frost a batch of these pumpkin-flavored cupcakes to take to a Halloween party. Make them look "hairy" by decorating with black shoelace licorice, or make eyes, noses, and mouths with candy corn.

For the cupcakes:
Nonstick cooking spray for greasing the tin
2 cups all-purpose flour
2 teaspoons baking powder
¼ teaspoon baking soda
½ cup firmly packed dark brown sugar
½ teaspoon salt
½ teaspoon ground cinnamon
¼ teaspoon ground nutmeg
½ cup chocolate chips or raisins
1 cup canned pumpkin
2 eggs
½ cup milk
¼ cup (½ stick) butter, melted and cooled

1. *Make the cupcakes:* Preheat the oven to 400°F and spray a 12-cup muffin tin with nonstick cooking spray.

2. Into a large bowl, sift the flour, baking powder, baking soda, brown sugar, salt, cinnamon, and nutmeg. Stir in the chocolate chips or raisins.

3. Place the canned pumpkin in a medium mixing bowl. Add the eggs, milk, and melted butter; beat well with an electric mixture set on medium speed. Fold the pumpkin mixture into the flour mixture just until well combined.

SHOESTRING LICORICE FOR "HAIR"

4. Spoon and scrape the batter into the prepared muffin tin. Bake on the center rack of the oven for 20 to 25 minutes, or until the cupcakes test done when pierced with a skewer. They should be golden brown. Cool in the tin for 2 minutes. Transfer to a rack to finish cooling.

5. *Make the icing:* In a medium mixing bowl, with an electric mixer set on medium speed, beat the cream cheese and butter for 1 minute. Add the vanilla; beat well. Add the confectioners' sugar and beat until smooth. Beat in a few drops of red and yellow food coloring. When the icing is the desired shade of orange, frost the cupcakes. Decorate as desired with the licorice or candy corn.

Thanksgiving

It's the quintessential American holiday, the one we all celebrate on the same day in the same way, no matter what our ethnic or religious background. It's Thanksgiving, a day for families and for feasting.

Feasting was also the order of the day at the very first Thanksgiving, which was held around 1621 in Plymouth, Massachusetts. After the first harvest, the Pilgrims invited the Native Americans to join them for a feast of thanksgiving that included deer, oysters, goose, duck, fruit, and cornmeal pudding.

More than a century later, President George Washington proclaimed November 26, 1789, to be a national Thanksgiving Day on which people would offer thanks and prayer. But the day was not accepted throughout our nation until 1863, when President Abraham Lincoln declared that Thanksgiving would be celebrated the last Thursday of each November. The holiday was officially moved to the fourth Thursday in November by President Franklin D. Roosevelt in 1941, and it's stayed this way ever since.

It's a day for visiting families, for getting dressed up, for setting a pretty table, and for savoring the mingling smells of turkey roasting and pie baking. Everyone eats until they can eat no more, and then, depending upon the individual family, people watch football on TV, relax, or play outside. In my family, all the cousins either play soccer or cheer on the players as we work up an appetite for dessert.

In this chapter I have included some traditional Thanksgiving sweets along with some that have become favorites in my own family.

Creamy Autumn-Apple Pie

SERVES 8

This is a nice twist on traditional apple pie, with a crust that's really simple to make.

1 recipe Oil Pie crust for a 2-crust pie (see following recipe)

2 pounds Granny Smith apples

¾ cup sugar plus 1 tablespoon sugar

2 tablespoons all-purpose flour

¾ teaspoon ground nutmeg

½ teaspoon ground cinnamon

Pinch of salt

¼ cup sour cream

1. Preheat the oven to 425°F. Prepare the pie crust. Line a 9-inch pie pan with half the dough. Peel, core, and slice the apples.

    USE A KNIFE OR A PEELER

2. In a small bowl, stir ¾ cup of the sugar, the flour, nutmeg, cinnamon, and salt. Sprinkle 2 tablespoons over the pie dough in the pie pan. Stir the remainder into the sour cream. Stir the sour cream into the sliced apples. Turn the apple mixture into the pie pan and spread evenly.

3. Roll out the remaining dough. Cut it into long strips and crisscross them over the top of the pie to form a lattice top. Moisten the edges with water to join the strips to the bottom crust. Sprinkle the remaining 1 tablespoon sugar over the top.

4. Bake the pie for 15 minutes. Reduce the oven to 325°F, and bake 45 minutes longer, or until the apples are tender and the crust is golden brown. Cool for 2 hours.

☆ Oil Pie crust

2 cups all-purpose flour
1 teaspoon salt
½ cup vegetable oil
¼ cup cold milk
Flour for the work
   surface and rolling pin

1. In a mixing bowl, stir the flour and salt. Add the oil and the milk; stir until moistened. Divide the dough into 2 equal balls.

2. Sprinkle the work surface and rolling pin with some flour. Roll out 1 ball of dough large enough to line a 9-inch pie pan. You'll use the other portion for the criss-cross topping.

WEAVE STRIPS OF PIE CRUST DOUGH FOR THE TOP

OVER AND UNDER

TRIM ENDS

Molly's Light Pumpkin Pie

SERVES 6–8

My daughter Molly has had insulin-dependent diabetes since age nine, so she's not supposed to eat too much sugar. Every day she pricks her finger many times to check her blood sugar, and she takes about eight injections of insulin daily. She loves to cook and bake, and from seventh grade until her sophomore year in college, she wrote a biweekly column in the New York Daily News called "Kids in the Kitchen." On holidays at least one of our desserts is low in sugar so Molly can eat dessert, too. This is one of everyone's favorites.

2 eggs, lightly beaten
1 (16-ounce) can pumpkin puree
½ cup Splenda
½ teaspoon salt
1 teaspoon ground cinnamon
½ teaspoon ground ginger
¼ teaspoon ground cloves
1 teaspoon vanilla extract
1 (12-ounce) can evaporated skim milk
1 (8-inch) Lean Pie Crust (see following recipe)
Fat-free whipped topping (optional)

1. Preheat the oven to 425°F.

2. In a large bowl, combine the eggs, pumpkin, and Splenda. With an electric mixer set on medium speed, beat 1 minute. Add the salt, cinnamon, ginger, cloves, vanilla, and skim milk. Beat another minute or until smooth.

3. Pour the pumpkin custard into the pie crust. Bake for 15 minutes. Reduce the oven to 350°F and bake the pie for 45 minutes more or until a knife inserted near the center comes out clean. Cool to room temperature before serving. If you like, serve with a dollop of fat-free whipped topping. Refrigerate leftovers.

Extra Lean Pie Crust
MAKES 1 (8-INCH) PIE CRUST

½ cup sifted all-purpose flour

¼ teaspoon baking powder

¼ teaspoon salt

¼ cup light butter or margarine, at room temperature

Flour for the work surface

1. In a large bowl, stir together the flour, baking powder, and salt. Cut in the butter with a fork or pastry blender. Continue mixing until no pastry sticks to the sides of the bowl. Shape into a ball. Wrap and refrigerate for 1 hour.

2. On a lightly floured work surface, roll out the dough. Fit into an 8-inch pie pan.

ROLL OUT A PIE CRUST

ROLL HALF OF CIRCLE ONTO ROLLING PIN

TRANSFER TO PIE PAN

EASING INTO BOTTOM OF PIE PAN

Cinderella's Classic Pumpkin Pie

This pie is creamy, custardy, and perfectly spiced with cinnamon, ginger, and cloves. You'll have an extra pie crust when you make the recipe for Easiest Ever Pie Crust. Freeze for up to three months, or use for another pie.

½ recipe Easiest Ever
  Pie crust (see below)
2 eggs
1½ cups canned
  pumpkin puree
1½ cups canned
  evaporated milk
½ cup granulated sugar
½ cup firmly packed
  brown sugar
½ teaspoon salt
2 teaspoons ground
  cinnamon
½ teaspoon ground
  ginger
¼ teaspoon ground
  cloves
¼ cup milk

1. Preheat the oven to 425°F. Line a 9-inch pie pan with the pie crust dough. Prick the bottom several times with the tines of a fork.

2. In a large mixing bowl, beat the eggs with an electric mixer set on medium speed for a minute. Add the pumpkin, evaporated milk, both sugars, salt, cinnamon, ginger, cloves, and milk. Beat for about 2 minutes or until smooth.

3. Pour the filling into the prepared pie crust. Bake for 10 minutes. Reduce the oven temperature to 300°F and continue to bake the pie for 45 to 55 minutes, until the filling is set in the middle. If the pie crust starts to turn too dark during the baking time, cover the edges of the pie with aluminum foil.

4. Remove the pie from the oven and let it cool for at least 1 hour before serving. Be sure to refrigerate leftovers.

Easiest Ever Pie Crust

This is the recipe my mother used whenever she made pies. It remains my favorite all-time pie crust.

2¼ cups sifted all-purpose flour
1 teaspoon salt
¾ cup vegetable shortening
⅓ cup water
Flour for the work surface and rolling pin

1. In a large bowl, combine 2 cups of the flour and the salt. Cut in the shortening with your fingers until the mixture resembles coarse crumbs.

2. In a small bowl, stir the remaining ¼ cup flour into the water. With a fork, stir the flour-water paste into the flour-shortening mixture to form a dough.

3. Turn the dough out onto a lightly floured work surface and knead with the heel of your hand for 1 minute. If the mixture seems dry, add a few more drops water. Form 2 balls.

4. Roll out 1 ball of dough on the floured work surface. Carefully fit it into the pie pan. Repeat with remaining ball of dough. Or freeze this ball of dough for up to two months. You will probably have enough bits of dough left over for cutting out little pumpkins, hearts, or whatever other shape you want. Place these little cut-outs on the pumpkin custard before placing the pie in the oven.

Creamy Pumpkin Cheesecake with Cranberry Glaze

This is a glorious holiday dessert that combines two fall favorites: pumpkin and cranberries. Even kids who don't ordinarily like cheesecake like this.

Butter for greasing the pan
⅓ cup graham cracker crumbs
1 pound cream cheese, at room temperature
1 pint sour cream
4 eggs
½ teaspoon ground nutmeg
1 teaspoon ground cinnamon
1 cup sugar
1¾ cups pumpkin puree
Cranberry Glaze (see following recipe)

1. Preheat the oven to 325°F. Generously butter a 10-inch springform pan. Sprinkle it with the graham cracker crumbs.

2. In a large bowl, with an electric mixer set on low speed, beat the cream cheese, sour cream, eggs, nutmeg, cinnamon, and sugar. Beat 1 minute. Add the pumpkin and beat for 30 seconds.

3. Spoon and scrape the mixture into the pan. Bake for about 1 hour and 30 to 40 minutes, until a knife inserted in the center comes out clean.

4. Remove from the oven. After 10 minutes, loosen the springform part of the pan and remove it. Cool the cake on a rack. When thoroughly cool, paint with Cranberry Glaze. Store in the refrigerator.

Cranberry Glaze

MAKES ENOUGH FOR 1 CAKE

- **1 cup fresh cranberries**
- **2 tablespoons red currant jelly**
- **2 tablespoons cranberry-raspberry or cranberry-apple cocktail**
- **2 tablespoons orange juice**
- **3 tablespoons sugar**

1. In a small saucepan, combine all ingredients and bring to a boil over medium heat. Reduce the heat to low and simmer, stirring, for about 10 minutes or until the berries start to burst. Remove from the heat and allow to cool.

2. Using a spatula, spread glaze on top of the cheesecake.

Note: If you like, arrange waxed paper strips around edges of cake plate. Remove strips after you glaze the cake.

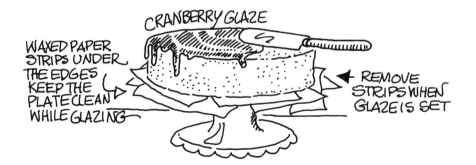

CRANBERRY GLAZE

WAXED PAPER STRIPS UNDER THE EDGES KEEP THE PLATE CLEAN WHILE GLAZING

REMOVE STRIPS WHEN GLAZE IS SET

Holiday Cream and Fruit Salad

If you don't like cranberries, just leave them out of this fresh, pretty salad. Add the bananas and whipped cream shortly before serving.

2 cups seedless green grapes
1 (12-ounce) bag fresh cranberries
6 large oranges
10 ounces pitted dates
1 cup heavy cream
2 tablespoons sugar
2 teaspoons vanilla extract
2 bananas

1. Wash, dry, and halve the grapes. Place in a large bowl; set aside.

2. Rinse and drain the cranberries. Pick over the berries, removing any stems or soft berries. Rinse and dry 1 orange; cut into 8 wedges.

3. In the work bowl of a food processor, combine the cranberries and the orange wedges. Process until finely chopped. Scrape the chopped fruit into another large bowl.

4. Slice the dates and add them to the cranberry bowl. Cover and refrigerate for about 1 hour.

5. Peel the remaining oranges. Divide into segments. Cut each segment in half crosswise. Add the orange segments to the halved grapes. Cover and refrigerate.

6. Shortly before serving, whip the heavy cream with an electric mixer set on high speed until soft peaks form. Add the sugar and the vanilla and beat just until stiff peaks form. Don't overbeat.

7. Stir the orange segments and grapes into the cranberry mixture with a rubber spatula. Peel the bananas and cut into chunks. Add the banana chunks to the fruit. Spoon into pretty dessert bowls and top each with a spoonful of whipped cream.

HEAVY CREAM

PROPERLY WHIPPED CREAM MAKES PEAKS

DO NOT OVERBEAT. TEST OFTEN.

Pumpkin Ice Cream Pie

If dessert isn't dessert without ice cream, this pie is for you!

⅓ **cup sugar**

1 cup canned pumpkin puree

½ **teaspoon ground cinnamon**

¼ **teaspoon ground ginger**

1 quart vanilla ice cream, slightly softened

1 (9-inch) graham cracker pie crust

Crushed graham cracker or gingersnap crumbs (optional)

1. In a medium mixing bowl, stir together the sugar, pumpkin, cinnamon, and ginger. Stir in the ice cream. You can use an electric mixer or an egg beater to beat in the ice cream.

EGG BEATER

2. Spoon the mixture into the pie crust. Cover with plastic wrap. Place in the freezer for 3 hours or overnight. Thaw for 10 minutes. If you like, sprinkle some graham cracker crumbs or gingersnap crumbs on top of the pie before you cut it into wedges and serve.

Spiced Thanksgiving Cider

SERVES 8

On a chilly November day, guests love to be handed a steaming mug of this cider. If you have a crockpot, you can keep the cider hot for hours. It's also excellent cold.

1 lemon
4 cups apple juice
1 cup water
**2 cups cranberry juice
cocktail or cranberry-
apple juice**
8 whole cloves
2 cinnamon sticks

1. Slice the lemon very thinly and set it aside.

2. In a large saucepan, stir together the apple juice, water, cranberry juice cocktail, cloves, and cinnamon sticks. Heat over medium heat, stirring occasionally, until steaming hot.

3. Strain the cider into another bowl to remove the cloves and the cinnamon sticks. Serve warm, garnished with lemon slices.

FLOAT A LEMON SLICE

Diwali

The colorful five-day Indian festival known as Diwali honors Hindu gods and goddesses and signals the beginning of winter. Also called the "Festival of Lights," Diwali represents the triumph of good over evil. In India on this holiday, homes glow with small earthen lamps, called "dipa," that are lit to welcome Lakshmi, the goddess of prosperity, and to help her find her way inside. The lamps are orange, the color that signifies good luck and wealth. Sometimes strings of lights are arranged so that they outline houses and buildings.

People clean their houses, decorate with flowers, and set up small altars with offerings of flowers and sweets. There are parades, firecrackers, musicians, and snake charmers, and, of course, there's plenty to eat. Sweets and snacks are prepared for friends and neighbors. Indian people eat so many of these treats that they're not that hungry for a big meal, so the emphasis at Diwali is not on enormous family feasts.

Indian cooks like to use lots of spices and nuts in their desserts. Indian sweets often contain honey, almonds, and pistachios.

India is the world's second largest rice grower, right after China. People in India eat about 160 pounds of rice per year. So it's no surprise that Indians like desserts made with rice. One of the most popular is Khir, a rice pudding that is very creamy and scented with rose water.

When I was looking for recipes for this chapter, I consulted my friend Anjali Roye, whose family comes from India. She helpfully provided me with some recipes that her mother likes to prepare at Diwali. Julie Sahni, a highly respected cooking teacher and cookbook author who I've known for a very long time, also gave me some of her favorite dessert recipes.

Khir

(Indian Rice Pudding)

This creamy, aromatic pudding is best served chilled.

½ cup rice
1 (2-inch) stick of cinnamon
4 whole cloves
4 cups milk
¾ cup firmly packed light brown sugar
4 cardamom pods
½ cup raisins
¼ cup chopped almonds
½ teaspoon rose water

1. Place the rice in a saucepan. Pour in enough water to cover and bring to a boil over medium heat. Add the cinnamon and cloves. Cover and simmer for 20 minutes or until the rice is soft.

2. Drain off any excess water from the rice. Stir in the milk and bring the mixture to a boil. Stir in the brown sugar.

3. Remove the husks from the cardamoms pods and add the seeds to the rice. Continue to simmer, stirring the rice to prevent it from sticking to the pan, 35 to 40 minutes, until the mixture has thickened.

4. Remove the cinnamon stick and the cloves. Add the raisins and almonds. Cover and simmer over very low heat for another 10 to 20 minutes, stirring often, until pudding is creamy.

5. Stir in the rose water. Allow the pudding to cool to room temperature, then cover and refrigerate for 2 to 3 hours, until cold.

Shrikhand

(Sweet Yogurt with Saffron)

This tastes a little bit different from the yogurt you're used to eating. It comes from central India and is the creation of Vandana Naik, the chef at Thom restaurant in New York City. Be sure to start making it at least several hours before you want to eat it, because the yogurt needs time to drain.

---

2 tablespoons raw pistachio nuts
2½ cups plain yogurt
¼ teaspoon saffron threads
1 tablespoon warm milk
½ cup sugar
¼ teaspoon ground cardamom

---

1. Coarsely chop the pistachios in a food processor; set aside.

2. Spoon the yogurt into a coffee filter set inside a large strainer. Place the strainer in a large bowl. Allow the yogurt to drain in the refrigerator for 4 or 5 hours. Discard the liquid.

3. In a small bowl, soak the saffron in the milk for 10 minutes.

4. In a mixing bowl, whisk together the drained yogurt, sugar, saffron milk, and cardamom. The mixture should be smooth and creamy.

5. Spoon into a serving bowl, cover with plastic wrap, and chill for 2 hours or until set. Garnish with the chopped pistachios.

YOGURT
COFFEE FILTER
STRAINER
YOGURT MUST DRAIN 4-5 HOURS

Vermicelli Milk Pudding

This sweet dessert is very similar to khir, *an Indian milk pudding made with rice.*

2½ ounces vermicelli
4 tablespoons sugar
4 cardamom pods
1 bay leaf
4 cups low-fat milk
3 tablespoons raisins
3 tablespoons slivered
   almonds
½ cup canned
   evaporated milk
Dash of freshly grated
   nutmeg

1. Break the vermicelli into pieces with your fingers. In a large saucepan, combine the sugar and the vermicelli.

2. Split open the cardamom pods. Scrape the small black seeds into the saucepan; discard the outer shells.

3. Add the bay leaf and the milk to the pan and bring to a boil, stirring occasionally. Reduce the heat and simmer the pudding, stirring every 5 minutes, for 15 minutes. Watch carefully to make sure it doesn't boil over.

4. Add the raisins, almonds, and evaporated milk. Remove the bay leaf.

5. Spoon the pudding into a pretty glass serving bowl. Cover with plastic wrap and chill in the refrigerator. Sprinkle the top of the pudding with freshly grated nutmeg before serving.

NUTMEG ON TOP

Suji Halwa

(Semolina Pudding)

This dessert, which is richer than the preceding puddings, will keep in a covered container in the refrigerator for a couple of weeks.

Butter for greasing the
   baking dish
2 cups milk
¾ cup semolina
2¼ cups firmly packed
   light brown sugar
¼ cup (½ stick) butter
10 cardamom pods
1 tablespoon chopped
   almonds

1. Lightly butter a 9 by 13-inch baking dish.

2. In a large saucepan, bring the milk to a boil. While it is heating up, stir 2 tablespoons of the milk into the semolina to make a thick paste, then add a few more tablespoons of milk. Spoon the semolina paste into the warm milk and stir well. Add the sugar and stir until it has dissolved. Remove the milk mixture from the heat.

3. In a sauté pan, heat the butter over low heat. Remove the seeds from the cardamom pods and crush them with a rolling pin. Add the seeds and the chopped almonds to the sauté pan and fry for 1 or 2 minutes. Pour the butter-cardamom mixture into the milk mixture and simmer over very low heat, stirring constantly to prevent the mixture from sticking to the saucepan.

4. When the mixture is very thick, spoon and scrape it into the prepared dish. Smooth the top and set aside to cool. When it is cool, cut into diamonds.

Pista Burfi

(Pistachio Fudge)

This isn't as sweet as American fudge—and it's not chocolate, either. You'll love the nutty taste.

Butter for greasing the
  baking pan
2 cups unsalted raw
  blanched pistachios
2 cups milk
¾ cup superfine sugar
1 tablespoon unsalted
  butter
¼ teaspoon almond
  extract

1. Butter a 7- or 8-inch square pan. Place the pistachios in a food processor and process until they are finely ground. Don't overprocess, or the pistachios will turn oily.

2. In a large, heavy, nonstick saucepan, stir together the milk and sugar. Cook, stirring, until the mixture comes to a boil. Continue to cook, stirring, over moderate heat until the mixture has reduced to about ½ cup. This will take about 20 minutes or more.

3. Reduce the heat and add the ground pistachios, butter, and almond extract. Cook until the mixture forms a soft ball that pulls away from the sides of the pan.

4. Spoon and scrape the fudge into the prepared pan, pressing down so that it is even. When it is cool, cut into squares with a sharp knife. Store in a covered container in the refrigerator for up to 2 weeks.

Apricot Fool

(Khoobani)

A fool is a funny name for a dessert, right? It's a very old-fashioned pudding that contains pureed fruit folded into whipped cream. You can make it with many different kinds of fruit. This recipe is from my friend Julie Sahni, whose wonderful books on Indian cooking contain great desserts.

12 dried apricots

½ cup water

10 gingersnaps

¾ cup heavy cream, chilled

4 tablespoons confectioners' sugar

APRICOT FOOL!

1. Combine the apricots and water in a 1-cup glass measure. Heat in the microwave, uncovered, on High for 1 minute or until the water boils. Remove from the microwave oven.

2. Pour the water and apricots into the container of a blender or food processor and process until smooth. Transfer the puree to a bowl and cover with plastic wrap. Refrigerate until thoroughly chilled, about 4 hours.

3. Crush the gingersnaps in a blender or food processor until finely ground. Remove to a bowl and set aside.

4. Remove the apricot puree from the refrigerator. In a large mixing bowl, with an electric mixer set on high speed, beat the cream with the confectioners' sugar until stiff peaks form. Reserve 2 tablespoons of the whipped cream for a garnish. Gently fold the whipped cream into the chilled apricot puree.

5. Spoon the mixture into 4 parfait glasses. Sprinkle the tops with the ground gingersnaps and garnish with the reserved whipped cream. Serve immediately.

Mata Srikhand

(Yogurt Cheese Dessert with Saffron)

This creamy dessert is also from Julie Sahni. You can eat it immediately or make it and keep in the refrigerator until dessert time. Saffron is a very expensive spice, but you only need a little bit. It is actually the yellow-orange stigmas from a small purple flower called a crocus.

¼ **teaspoon saffron threads**
2 **tablespoons boiling water**
6 **ounces cream cheese, at room temperature**
¾ **cup confectioners' sugar**
1 **cup plain yogurt**
¼ **teaspoon freshly grated nutmeg**
20 **seedless green or red grapes**

1. In a small bowl, soak the saffron threads in the boiling water for 10 minutes.

2. In a mixing bowl, with an electric mixer set on medium speed, beat the cream cheese and sugar for 2 minutes or until light. Stir in the saffron, yogurt, nutmeg, and 16 grapes. Spoon into 4 dessert dishes and garnish with the remaining 4 grapes. Serve immediately or refrigerate to serve later.

Ilaichi Biskoot

(Lemon Cardamom Cookies)

Try these for an after-school snack when you're in the mood for something a little exotic. Aromatic cardamom, a spice native to India, is a member of the ginger family.

1¼ cups all-purpose flour
1½ teaspoons ground cardamom
¾ teaspoon baking powder
¼ teaspoon kosher salt
½ cup (1 stick) unsalted butter, at room temperature
¾ cup sugar
1 large egg
1 teaspoon vanilla extract
1 teaspoon lemon juice
1 teaspoon grated lemon rind

1. Preheat the oven to 350°F.

2. Into a large mixing bowl, sift the flour, cardamom, baking powder, and salt.

3. In a medium mixing bowl, with an electric mixer set on medium speed, cream the butter and sugar for 2 or 3 minutes or until light. Add the egg, vanilla, lemon juice, and lemon rind and beat until fluffy.

4. Drop the batter by heaping teaspoonsful about 1½ inches apart onto an ungreased baking sheet. Bake 12 to 15 minutes or until lightly browned.

5. Allow the cookies to cool on the baking sheets for 1 minute before transferring them to a rack to finish cooling.

Chanukah

Right around the time of year when Christians celebrate Christmas, Jewish people celebrate Chanukah, an eight-day festival that commemorates the victory of Judah the Maccabee over the Syrians and the Greeks, and the rededication of the temple in Jerusalem. The holiday, known as the Festival of Lights, which falls in November or December, is a warm and happy time, with lighted candles that chase away the winter chill and games and treats for children. Kids have fun playing a game of chance with a *dreidel*, a top with four sides. Each side is inscribed with a Hebrew letter. Kids of all ages spin the *dreidel* and try to win pennies, nuts, or candy.

The story of Chanukah is very interesting. More than two thousand years ago, the Jews, led by Judah the Maccabee, were fighting to drive the Syrian armies out of Israel. After Judah had defeated the tyrant Antiochus, the Jews reclaimed the temple in Jerusalem, which had been desecrated. Everyone was busy scrubbing and cleaning so that services could begin again, but there was only enough pure oil to allow the menorah (an eight-branched candelabra) to burn for twenty-four hours. Miraculously, the menorah stayed lit for eight days and nights, until more oil could be obtained.

During Chanukah, Jewish families light a menorah in their homes on each of the eight nights, to commemorate the Maccabees' fight for freedom and the miracle of the oil. Each night they light another candle in the menorah, and everyone gathers around to sing "Rock of Ages" ("Maoz Tsur"), which is a famous hymn of praise.

Because of the Chanukah miracle in which the oil lamp burned much longer than it was supposed to, traditional holiday foods are made with oil. In Israel, people love to eat jelly doughnuts, called "sufganiyot." Ashkenazic Jews enjoy potato pancakes, called "latkes," as a traditional holiday treat. Potato latkes taste best when they are crisp and greaseless, and when they're served with the classic accompaniments of applesauce and sour cream. Latkes can be made with other vegetables, too. Carrots and zucchini both work very well in these pancakes. Traditionally, latkes aren't eaten as a dessert but I've included a recipe because kids love them. Also included here are the sweets that are popular at Chanukah.

Classic Potato Latkes

SERVES 4–6

Be sure to let the grated potatoes drain briefly but thoroughly before you use them. Serve with sour cream and applesauce.

4 large potatoes
½ onion
2 eggs
1 teaspoon salt
4 tablespoons self-rising flour
Vegetable oil for frying

1. Line a large tray with paper towels. Peel the potatoes and grate them, either by hand or in a food processor. Set aside in a sieve to drain for 10 or 15 minutes. Meanwhile, peel and chop the onion. In a small bowl, lightly beat the eggs.

2. Place the drained potato in a large mixing bowl. Stir in the chopped onion, lightly beaten eggs, salt, and flour. Stir very well.

3. Pour enough vegetable oil into a heavy frying pan to reach a depth of ½ inch and heat over medium heat. When the oil is hot, scoop tablespoonsful of the potato mixture into the pan and cook over medium heat for about 5 minutes, flattening the latkes with the back of a spoon. Turn and cook on the other side until golden brown. Transfer the latkes to the paper towel–lined tray to drain.

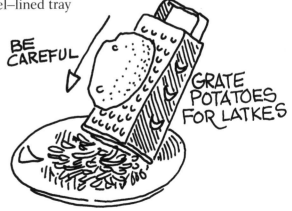

BE CAREFUL

GRATE POTATOES FOR LATKES

Sweet-Potato Latkes

SERVES 4–6

There is a hint of fresh ginger in these naturally sweet latkes, which reheat very nicely. Serve them with homemade applesauce. If you have a food processor, this recipe is incredibly easy. You can freeze these pancakes for up to a month, on a baking sheet in a single layer. To reheat, place them on a baking sheet in a preheated 400°F oven for 8 to 12 minutes, until crisp.

2 medium sweet
  potatoes
I small piece (about
  I by 2 inches) fresh
  ginger
2 eggs
½ cup milk
½ cup all-purpose flour
I tablespoon sugar
I teaspoon baking
  powder
¾ teaspoon salt
Vegetable oil for frying
Applesauce or maple
  syrup

1. Line a large tray with paper towels. Peel the potatoes and grate them by hand or shred them with the shredding disk of a food processor. Transfer the potatoes to a large mixing bowl.

2. Peel the ginger and finely chop it. You should have about 2 tablespoons of ginger. Stir it into the potatoes.

3. In a medium mixing bowl, combine the eggs, milk, flour, sugar, baking powder, and salt. Beat until smooth. (If you have a food processor, use it for this step.)

4. Add the milk mixture to the potatoes. Stir and toss to blend.

5. Pour enough oil into a large heavy skillet to reach a depth of 1 inch and heat over medium-high heat. When the oil is very hot, scoop ⅓ cupful of batter into the skillet. The latkes should be 3 or 4 inches in diameter. Cook several minutes, until golden on the bottom. Turn and cook 4 minutes on the other side. Transfer the latkes to the paper towel–lined tray to drain. Keep making latkes until all the batter is used up. Serve warm, with applesauce or maple syrup.

Sweet Carrot Pancakes

SERVES 4–6

These are delicious for brunch in place of potato latkes, though you could also serve them for dinner. They are just a little spicy, and crunchy from the walnuts.

1 pound carrots
1 egg
1 tablespoon lemon juice
3 tablespoons sugar
½ teaspoon ground cinnamon
Pinch of nutmeg
¾ to 1 cup whole-wheat flour
½ cup chopped walnuts (optional)
3 tablespoons vegetable oil
3 tablespoons unsalted butter
Brown sugar for topping

1. Peel the carrots and grate them in a food processor or by hand. In a large mixing bowl, beat the egg. Add the carrots, lemon juice, sugar, cinnamon, and nutmeg. Stir vigorously to blend.

2. Stir in enough flour to create a fairly thick batter. You want to be able to form pancakes by hand. Stir in the nuts, if using.

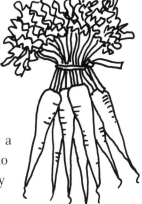

3. In a large, heavy skillet, heat half the oil with half the butter over medium heat. Form pancakes that are 2 to 3 inches in diameter. Fry until golden brown, then turn and fry on the other side. Drain on paper towels. Wipe out the pan. Heat the remaining oil and butter. Continue frying pancakes until the remaining batter is used up. Drain briefly. Sprinkle the pancakes with the brown sugar and serve warm.

Fudgy Chanukah Gelt

These holiday candies make a nice gift. They're rich, fudgy, and creamy all at the same time.

Butter for greasing the
  baking sheet
1 pound (1 box)
  confectioners' sugar
1 pound semisweet
  chocolate, broken into
  pieces
½ cup unsweetened
  cocoa powder
¼ teaspoon salt
6 tablespoons (¾ stick)
  margarine
5 tablespoons milk
1 teaspoon vanilla
  extract

1. Lightly butter a baking sheet. In the top of a double boiler over simmering water, combine all the ingredients. Stir and cook until smooth.

2. Spread mixture evenly on the prepared baking sheet. Allow to cool.

3. Cut out gelt with a Chanukah cookie cutter. Place on a plate and refrigerate until serving time.

Israeli Doughnuts

(Sufganiyot)

These doughnuts must be deep fried, which is definitely something a grown-up should do because hot oil can be extremely dangerous. Once the doughnuts are ready, you can dip them into the warm honey syrup before you eat them.

1½ cups all-purpose flour
½ cup warm water
1 package active dry yeast
1 egg
¼ teaspoon salt
½ cup sugar
½ tablespoon oil
Oil for deep frying
Honey Syrup (see following recipe)

1. Line a large tray with paper towels. Sift the flour into a large bowl. Pour ¼ cup of the warm water into a small bowl. Stir the yeast into the water and mix until it has dissolved. Add the egg, salt, sugar, and ½ tablespoon oil. Stir to combine.

2. Pour the yeast mixture into the flour mixture and mix well. Add the remaining ¼ cup warm water and mix well. You should have a sticky dough. Stir in a little bit more flour if it seems too sticky. Cover the bowl with a dish towel and allow it to rise for 1 hour in a warm place.

3. The next steps are definitely for a grownup. Pour enough oil into a large deep pot to reach a depth of 3 inches and heat to 375°F or until little bubbles rise to the surface. Dip a spoon into the oil. Then scoop up a tablespoon of dough and gently put it into the pot. Be careful that the oil doesn't splash. You should cook just a few *sufganiyot* at a time. They will puff up and float.

4. Turn the *sufganiyot* with a slotted spoon and fry until golden. Transfer to the paper towel–lined tray. Continue until all the dough is used. Dip the *sufganiyot* in the Honey Syrup while still warm, or serve the syrup on the side.

Honey Syrup

MAKES ENOUGH FOR 20 *SUFGANIYOT*

½ cup honey
3 tablespoons water
¼ teaspoon ground
cinnamon

In a small saucepan, heat all the ingredients over low heat until well combined. Pour the syrup into a small bowl or pitcher.

Cookie Lover's Rugelach

MAKES 4 DOZEN
SMALL PASTRIES

These tender crescent-shaped cookies are a universal favorite. The dough is very easy to work with. If you prefer, use strawberry jam.

For the dough:
1 cup (2 sticks) butter, at room temperature
8 ounces cream cheese, at room temperature
2 tablespoons sugar
1/4 teaspoon salt
2 cups all-purpose flour plus extra for work surface

For the filling:
1 cup finely chopped walnuts
1/2 cup brown sugar
1 teaspoon ground cinnamon
1 cup raspberry jam

1. *Make the dough*: In a mixing bowl, with an electric mixer set on medium speed, beat the butter, cream cheese, and sugar for 2 minutes, until light and fluffy. Add the salt. Beat in the 2 cups flour in 2 additions. Divide the dough into 4 equal portions. Form into balls, wrap, and refrigerate overnight.

2. Preheat the oven to 375°F. On a lightly floured work surface, using a rolling pin, roll out each piece of dough into a 1/8-inch round that is about 14 inches in diameter.

4. *Make the filling*: In a bowl, combine the walnuts, brown sugar, and cinnamon.

5. Brush the dough rounds very lightly with the raspberry jam, leaving about a 1/2-inch border around the edges. Sprinkle evenly with the nut mixture. Cut each round into 12 wedges. Roll up the wedges from the wide end toward the point. Pinch the point to seal. Bend ends gently to form crescents. Place on ungreased baking sheets.

6. Bake for 15 to 20 minutes, or until golden brown. Let the pastries cool for about 1 minute, until firm. Transfer to a rack to cool completely. These will keep for a week at room temperature, or they may be frozen for up to two months.

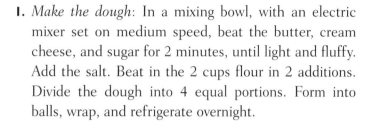

Apple Dapple Cinnamon Applesauce

SERVES 8

This is the best applesauce to serve with potato latkes. It's got a little cinnamon in it, plus raisins, which you can leave out if you don't like them.

1 large lemon
8 large apples
½ cup maple syrup
2 cinnamon sticks
¼ cup raisins
2 tablespoons brown
   sugar

1. Cut the lemon into quarters. Peel, core, and quarter the apples.

2. In a large pot, combine the apple quarters, maple syrup, cinnamon sticks, and raisins. Add the lemon wedges and stir. Sprinkle with the brown sugar and bring to a boil. Reduce the heat and simmer, partially covered, for 15 to 20 minutes, stirring occasionally, until the apples are soft.

3. Discard the cinnamon sticks and the lemon wedges. Mash the applesauce with a fork until chunky. Serve hot or cold.

Maple-Baked Apples

SERVES 4

The best apples to use for this delicious dessert are ones that hold their shape, such as Rome Beauties. Try not to use McIntosh apples, which are so juicy they get mushy in the oven. If you like, drizzle a little heavy cream over the baked apples before you serve them.

4 apples
4 tablespoons brown sugar
1 teaspoon ground cinnamon
4 tablespoons raisins
4 tablespoons chopped walnuts
1 lemon
½ cup pure maple syrup

1. Preheat the oven to 375°F. Hollow out the cores of the apples without cutting all the way through. Do not peel the apples. Leave them whole.

2. Arrange the apples in a large glass baking dish. Into the hollowed-out core of each apple, spoon 1 tablespoon brown sugar, ¼ teaspoon cinnamon, 1 tablespoon raisins, and 1 tablespoon chopped walnuts.

3. Squeeze the lemon over the apples, then drizzle them with maple syrup. Fill the bottom of the baking dish with about ½ inch of water.

4. Bake for 45 minutes or until the apples are soft in the center but retain their shape. Serve warm.

Christmas

The magical holiday of Christmas, though officially just one day (December 25), really spills over into several weeks. It starts in our hearts right after Thanksgiving, when decorations appear overnight in city streets, town squares, houses, and apartment windows. Stores are packed with busy shoppers, and every imaginable toy you could ever wish for is on display. Festive music fills the air, and schools are busy preparing special programs for their bands, orchestras, and choruses.

Long before Christmas Eve, we're already feeling happy and full of anticipation. And annual rite in our house takes place when, on Thanksgiving night, I bring down the dozens of Christmas books that I store in my bedroom closet. We read the same ones aloud year after year so that we've practically memorized them. It's a cozy, close way to get ready for bed each night during this joyful season. Carols play in our house and in my car, and if we aren't anywhere I can play music, I sing. All my children have learned "Silent Night," "The First Noel," and "Oh Little Town of Bethlehem" by the time they reach kindergarten.

Santa Claus is a huge presence, of course, but my family tries to keep in sight the main reason we celebrate on this day. We are commemorating the birth of the baby Jesus on that first Christmas more than two thousand years ago. You might know this story well, but it's fun to hear it over and over. Mary and Joseph were traveling when it was time for Mary to have her baby. Although they tried to stop at an inn where she could give birth, they couldn't find one with a vacancy. And so the infant was born in a stable in Bethlehem and laid in a manger in a bed of straw. As the brilliant star of Bethlehem shone brightly, shepherds and angels came to worship the Christ Child in that humble place, home to donkeys and sheep.

During Advent, the period leading up to Christmas, Christians prepare their hearts for the coming of God. When I was growing up, we had an Advent crib, which was a big cylindrical oatmeal box that my father had decorated with colorful paper and glitter. Each time one of us did a good deed, we were allowed to place one piece of straw inside. We wanted the whole crib to be full by Christmas Eve, when we would gently lay the baby Jesus (a doll) into it. Of course, we didn't always agree on what constituted a good deed, and my mother was frequently called in to mediate a dispute!

Every night after dinner, we'd sit around the supper table and sing religious Christmas carols. Leading our chorus was my father, who has an excellent voice and is still a prominent member of his church choir.

On Christmas Eve, we'd form a procession and parade through our house, holding lit candles and singing Christmas songs. Betsy, the youngest child, got to place the figure of the baby Jesus into a nativity scene displayed in the living room. Barbara, the second youngest, placed a slightly larger doll in our Advent crib, which by that point was filled with pieces of straw, legitimately or illegitimately earned!

As the oldest child, I never got to lay a baby in the crib, but I did get to take a lead role in my mother's holiday baking sessions. We made platters and platters of decorated cookies and braided, yeast-raised coffee cakes swathed in white icing and topped with maraschino cherries. My grandmother's brown bread, sweetened with molasses and raisins, was made in great batches to be distributed to all our teachers.

For me, the most enjoyable baking project of this season is cookies. We no longer confine ourselves just to rolled cutouts but also whip up batches of cookies from other lands. Children of all ages love cookies, and nothing says Christmas better than a big plate with several different kinds arranged on it.

Melt-in-Your-Mouth Turkish Butter Cookies

(Kurabiye)

Be sure to coat these melt-in-your-mouth morsels with a shower of confectioners' sugar after baking so they're pure white.

- ½ cup confectioners' sugar plus extra for coating the cookies
- ½ teaspoon vanilla extract
- ½ cup (I stick) unsalted butter, at room temperature
- I cup all-purpose flour

1. Preheat the oven to 300°F. Position a rack in the middle of the oven. Line a baking sheet with parchment paper.

2. In a large mixing bowl, with an electric mixer set on medium speed, beat the sugar, vanilla, and butter for 2 or 3 minutes, until light and fluffy.

3. Measure the flour into a sifter. Sift it into the butter mixture in 3 additions, beating well after each.

3. Pat the dough into a rectangle. Cut the dough into 20 squares. Place the cookies 2 inches apart on the prepared baking sheet. Bake on the middle rack of the oven for 18 to 20 minutes, until golden.

4. Remove the cookies from the oven and with a spatula, transfer them to a wire rack.

5. Place confectioners' sugar on a shallow dinner plate. Coat the warm cookies with plenty of the sugar. Store in an airtight container.

Buttery German Spritz Cookies

MAKES ABOUT 5 DOZEN

You'll need a cookie press to make these buttery cookies. If you're going to form the dough into wreaths, tint it green before forming the wreaths and then decorate each cookie with red hots or red sprinkles before baking.

½ pound (2 sticks) unsalted butter, plus extra for greasing the baking sheets
½ cup sugar
¼ teaspoon salt
1 teaspoon vanilla extract
1 egg
2¼ cups sifted all-purpose flour
Sprinkles, jimmies, and red hots for decorating, if you like

1. Preheat the oven to 375°F. Lightly butter some baking sheets.

2. In a large mixing bowl, with an electric mixer set on medium speed, beat the butter for 2 minutes, until little tails form and it's pale yellow. Gradually add the sugar and beat until light and fluffy. Add the salt, vanilla, and egg. Beat until thoroughly combined.

3. Sift in half the flour and beat again. Sift in the remaining flour and stir vigorously with a wooden spoon until you have a nice soft dough. Tint with food coloring, if desired. Spoon the dough into a cookie press and pipe out cookies onto the prepared baking sheets. You can make wreaths, stars, candy canes, squiggles, or any shape you like. Press jimmies, sprinkles, or red hots into the tops of the cookies.

4. Bake for 8 to 10 minutes, until the edges of the cookies are golden. With a spatula, transfer the cookies to a wire rack to cool completely.

MIX WITH WOODEN SPOON

Happy Holiday Cookie Cutouts

MAKES 3 DOZEN

This is Basic Holiday Cookie Dough, and it makes many different kinds of cookies. You can double this recipe, depending upon how ambitious you feel. Choose cookie cutters shaped like bells, stars, gingerbread people, or Santas.

- 2 sticks (1 cup) unsalted butter, at room temperature
- 1 cup sugar
- 2 eggs
- 2 teaspoons vanilla extract
- 3 cups all-purpose flour, plus extra for the work surface
- ½ teaspoon baking soda
- ¾ teaspoon salt
- Nonstick cooking spray for greasing the baking sheets
- Vanilla Icing (see following recipe)

1. In a large bowl, with an electric mixer set on medium speed, beat the butter for 1 minute. Gradually add the sugar and beat until smooth. Beat in the eggs, one at a time. Beat in the vanilla.

2. Measure the flour into a large sifter set over a dinner plate. Add baking soda and salt. Sift flour mixture into the egg-butter mixture and beat on medium speed until smooth. If the dough seems sticky, beat in a few more tablespoons of flour.

3. Remove the dough from the bowl, form it into 3 balls, and wrap each in plastic. Refrigerate for at least 1 hour

WRAP DOUGH IN PLASTIC WRAP AND REFRIGERATE

or overnight. (The dough may also be frozen for up to 1 month.)

4. Preheat the oven to 375°F. When ready to bake, remove 1 dough ball at a time from the refrigerator and set it on the work surface for 5 minutes or until pliable. Knead it briefly with your hands if necessary until it is pliable. Spray a baking sheet with nonstick cooking spray. Lightly dust work surface with flour.

5. Roll out the dough to about a ⅛-inch thickness. Cut out cookies with a table knife or holiday cookie cutters. Reroll the scraps and cut out more cookies.

6. Place the cookies about 2 inches apart on the prepared baking sheet. Bake for 8 to 10 minutes, until the bottoms are just starting to brown and the tops are firm. With a spatula, transfer the cookies to a wire rack. Let cool about 25 minutes before icing with Vanilla Icing. Repeat with remaining dough.

Vanilla Icing

MAKES ENOUGH FOR 3–4 DOZEN COOKIES

This frosting is so versatile you'll use it on cupcakes and cakes, too. To vary the flavor, substitute lemon or almond extract for the vanilla extract.

3 cups confectioners' sugar
3 tablespoons butter, at room temperature
⅓ cup milk, plus more as needed
¾ teaspoon vanilla extract

In a large mixing bowl, combine all the ingredients. Beat well with an electric mixer set on high speed for about 2 minutes or until the icing is creamy and smooth. Use immediately or refrigerate in an airtight container for up to 3 days.

Christmas Tree Cookie Ornaments

MAKES 3 DOZEN

Thread ribbons through the holes and hang these on your Christmas tree.

1 batch Basic Holiday Cookie Dough (see page 233)
Nonstick cooking spray
Flour for dusting the work surface
1 batch Vanilla Icing (see page 235)
10–15 drops food coloring
Rainbow or chocolate sprinkles, chocolate chips, red hots, or similar candies

ICING HOLDS THE "RED HOT" DECORATIONS

1. Preheat the oven to 375°F. Remove 1 dough ball at a time from refrigerator and set on work surface for 5 minutes. Knead 4 or 5 times on work surface to soften. Spray a baking sheet with nonstick cooking spray. Lightly dust work surface with flour.

2. Roll out the dough to about a ¼-inch thickness. Cut out cookies with a round cookie cutter (a serrated one adds a fancy edge). Use a skewer to make a ¼-inch hole near the top of each cookie. Reroll scraps and cut out more cookies.

3. Place the cookies about two inches apart on the prepared baking sheet and bake for 8 to 10 minutes, until the bottoms are just starting to brown and the tops are firm. With a spatula, transfer the cookies to a wire rack. Let cool about 15 minutes. Repeat with remaining dough.

4. Tint the icing with food coloring of your choice (about 10 drops will lend a rich color) and ice each cookie. Top with sprinkles or candy. You can keep your work area neater by putting sprinkles, jimmies, and red hots into a muffin pan so that each one has its own little compartment. Allow the frosting to dry for at least 1 hour. Thread a ribbon through the hole in each cookie. Hang the cookie ornaments on your tree or store in an airtight container.

Peppermint Candy Cane Cookies

For an even more festive version, add green food coloring to half the dough and red to the other half.

I batch Basic Holiday Cookie Dough (divided into 2 balls before chilling), see page 233
Nonstick cooking spray for greasing baking sheet
10–15 drops red food coloring

1. Preheat the oven to 375°F. Remove dough from refrigerator and set on work surface for 5 minutes or until pliable. Knead it 4 or 5 times to soften. Lightly spray a baking sheet with cooking spray.

2. Add 10 drops red food coloring to 1 ball of dough and mix well; adjust amount depending upon how dark you want the red. Leave the other ball white.

3. Break off small pieces of red dough and roll into 5-inch lengths about as thick as a pencil. Repeat with the untinted dough. (If it's too sticky, add a couple of tablespoons of flour.) Starting at one end, twist a strand of red dough around a strand of untinted dough

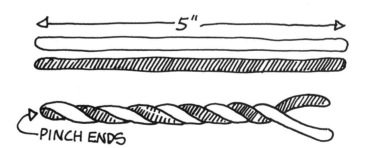

5"

PINCH ENDS

as though braiding the two. Pinch both ends together. Bend the twisted strands into a cane shape.

4. Carefully place canes on the prepared baking sheet, about 1 inch apart. Bake for 8 to 10 minutes, until lightly browned on the bottom. With a spatula, remove canes to a wire rack and let cool. Store in an airtight container with waxed paper between the layers.

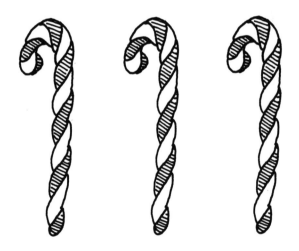

Stained-Glass Cookies

MAKES ABOUT 2 DOZEN

These sparkling gems make a nice addition to a plate of cookies that you plan to give to a neighbor. You could also make these into ornaments. Just use a skewer to make a hole near the top of each cookie before baking them.

½–1 cup red or green hard candies, such as Lifesavers

1 batch Basic Holiday Cookie Dough (see page 233)

Flour for dusting the rolling pin

Sugar for sprinkling on the cookies

1. Preheat the oven to 375°F. Line a large baking sheet with parchment paper.

2. In the work bowl of a food processor fitted with a metal blade, process the candies until they are finely ground. If you don't have a food processor, crush the candies with a mortar and pestle. Scrape the candy into a small bowl.

3. Remove the dough from the refrigerator and knead 4 or 5 times on the work surface to soften. With a lightly floured rolling pin, roll the dough out to a ⅛-inch thickness. With a small cookie cutter or biscuit cutter, cut the dough into 3-inch rounds. With a plastic knife, make a few cuts in the center of each cookie to leave a small cutout area about the size of a nickel. Place the cookies 2 inches apart on the prepared baking sheet.

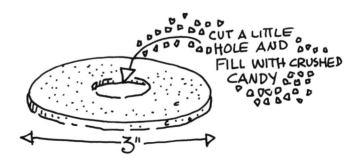

CUT A LITTLE HOLE AND FILL WITH CRUSHED CANDY

3"

4. With a small spoon, fill each cutout with candy. The candy should be level with the dough. Sprinkle the cookies with sugar. Repeat with remaining dough.

5. Bake for 8 to 10 minutes, or until the cookies are lightly browned on the bottom. Let cool for a few minutes on baking sheet before removing to a wire rack to cool completely. Store them in an airtight container.

Toffee Crinkles

MAKES ABOUT 3 DOZEN

You can substitute another candy bar, such as Snickers, but be sure to chop it finely before adding to the dough.

**1 cup Heath Bar chunks
1 recipe Basic Holiday Cookie Dough (see page 233)**

1. Preheat the oven to 375°F. Line a large baking sheet with parchment paper.

2. In a food processor fitted with the metal blade, finely chop the Heath Bar. Pour into a small bowl.

3. Remove dough from the refrigerator and knead it four or five times on the work surface to soften it. Sprinkle chopped Heath Bar over dough and work with your hands until it is thoroughly combined.

4. Roll dough into small balls about the size of a walnut. Place 2 inches apart on the prepared baking sheet. Bake for 8 minutes or until the cookies are lightly browned on the bottoms. Remove the cookies from the oven and let cool. Repeat with remaining dough, until all the dough is used up.

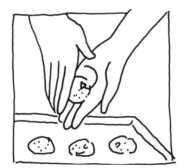

Mini Chocolate Sandwich Rounds

MAKES 1 DOZEN

Fill these versatile cookies with vanilla icing or peanut butter. Or if you really want to get into the holiday spirit, tint the vanilla icing red or green with a few drops of food color.

Nonstick cooking spray or parchment paper
½ recipe Basic Holiday Cookie Dough (see page 233)
Flour for dusting the rolling pin
½ recipe Vanilla Icing or ⅓ cup smooth peanut butter
1 (6-ounce) package semisweet chocolate chips

1. Preheat the oven to 375°F. Spray a large baking sheet with nonstick cooking spray or line it with parchment paper. Remove dough from the refrigerator and knead it 4 or 5 times on the work surface to soften it.

2. With a lightly floured rolling pin, roll out the dough to a ⅛-inch thickness. With a 3-inch round cookie cutter or biscuit cutter, cut the dough. Arrange the cookies about 1 inch apart on the prepared baking sheet.

3. Bake for 10 minutes or until lightly browned on the bottom and firm on the top. Remove from the cookie sheet with a spatula, and let cool on a wire rack. Repeat with remaining dough. When they're completely cool, spread icing on half the cookies; assemble sandwiches.

4. Place the chocolate chips in a shallow, microwave-proof bowl. Heat in the microwave oven on High for 1 minute and stir. Heat for 1½ to 2 minutes more, stirring in 30-second intervals, until melted. Dip the cookies in the melted chocolate, swirling to cover one end. Place cookies on waxed paper to dry and harden for 30 minutes.

Grandma's Brown Bread

This has been our breakfast on Christmas morning for as long as I can remember. My mother made it each year, and I helped make big batches to give as gifts. The bread is best spread with cream cheese, though it's also very good plain. You can make it ahead and store at room temperature for a week.

Cooking spray for the pans
1½ cups raisins
½ cup water
½ cup sugar
2 tablespoons butter
1 egg
2 tablespoons molasses
2¾ cups sifted all-purpose flour
2 teaspoons baking soda
½ teaspoon salt

1. Preheat the oven to 350°F. Lightly spray 2 (1-pound) coffee cans (or small loaf pans, if you don't have coffee cans) with cooking spray.

2. In a small saucepan, boil the raisins in the water for 1 minute. Set aside to cool.

3. In a mixing bowl, with an electric mixer set on medium speed, beat the sugar with the butter for 2 minutes. Add the egg and the molasses and beat for 1 minute.

4. Into a separate bowl, sift the flour, baking soda, and salt. Sift the flour mixture into the butter mixture and beat until thoroughly combined. Drain the raisins and add them to the batter.

5. Spoon and scrape the batter into the coffee cans. Bake for 50 minutes, or until a toothpick inserted into the center of a loaf comes out clean. Cool for 5 minutes in the pans. Remove to a rack and cool completely.

Stollen

A traditional sweet yeast bread that originated in Germany. Stollen is typically filled with dried fruit. This version is adapted from one that originally appeared in the New York Daily News in 1969. It is every bit as good today as it was then. This is a sweet treat to give as a gift at Christmas. You can also wrap the stollen well in plastic and freeze until needed.

Cooking spray for the
   bowl and baking
   sheets
3/4 cup raisins
1/2 cup slivered citron
1/4 cup chopped candied
   cherries
1/4 cup orange juice
5 to 6 cups unsifted all-
   purpose flour
1/2 cup sugar
1 teaspoon salt
2 packages active dry
   yeast
1 cup milk
3/4 cup (1 1/2 sticks)
   butter
3 eggs
1 teaspoon almond
   extract
3/4 cup finely chopped
   almonds

1. Spray a very large bowl and a large baking sheet with cooking spray; set aside. In another large bowl, place the raisins, citron, and candied cherries. Stir in the orange juice.

2. In a large mixing bowl, combine 2 cups of the flour, the sugar, salt, and yeast; set aside.

3. In a saucepan, heat the milk and butter over very low heat until almost blended and melted; set aside.

4. In a medium bowl, beat the eggs with an electric mixer set on medium speed. Add the almond extract, chopped almonds, and milk-butter mixture; stir well. Add this mixture gradually to the dry ingredients. Beat in enough additional flour to form a soft dough. Turn the dough out onto a floured work surface. Knead the dough, adding more flour if needed, until it is smooth and elastic.

5. Place the dough in the large greased bowl. Turn the dough over once to grease the top surface. Cover the dough with a clean cloth and allow it to rise in a warm spot for about 1 hour or until doubled in bulk. Punch the dough down. Turn it out onto a floured work surface. Knead in the fruit mixture.

3 tablespoons butter, melted
Confectioners' sugar for coating the loaves

6. Divide the dough into 3 equal parts. Pat each piece into an oval (12 by 7 inches). Fold each lengthwise, not quite in half so that the bottom edge extends 1 inch beyond the top. Pinch closed. Place the loaves on the prepared baking sheets. Brush with the melted butter, using about 1 tablespoon per loaf. Cover with a sheet of waxed paper, then with a clean cloth. Cover and let rise about 1 hour or until puffy.

7. Preheat the oven to 350°F. Bake the loaves for about 20 to 30 minutes or until nicely browned. Remove to racks. While they are warm, sift confectioners' sugar over the loaves until heavily coated.

Kwanzaa

The day after Christmas, a wonderful seven-day long festival called "Kwanzaa" begins. A chance for African Americans to reflect upon their culture and savor delicious foods, this relatively new holiday is celebrated from December 26 through New Year's Day.

Since Kwanzaa was created in 1966 by Dr. Maulana Karenga, it's become enormously popular and now is celebrated by millions of African-American families. The celebration focuses on seven principles that contribute to the unity of the black family and on how these can be applied to daily life. The principles are unity, self-determination, collective work and responsibility, cooperative economics, purpose, creativity, and faith.

Kwanzaa means "first fruits of the harvest," and in African-American households, a bowl of fruits and vegetables is likely to be arranged on the dining table, along with a straw place mat and a *kinara*, which is a seven-branched candelabra with black, red, and green candles. Children light the *kinara*, recite the seven principles, and help prepare special dishes. Very often these dishes are made with foods grown in Africa, such as peanuts. Coconut, sweet potatoes, and bananas often show up in the sweets that are eaten during this week-long festival.

Chocolate–Peanut Cookie "Pizza"

SERVES 6 TO 8

My friend Joyce White, who wrote a book called Soul Food: Recipes and Reflections from African American Churches, *likes to make chocolate- and peanut-topped sugar cookies for Kwanzaa. Instead of individual sugar cookies, I experimented with a cookie pizza and all my "cookie monsters" loved it.*

For the pizza:
⅓ cup butter, at room temperature
⅓ cup vegetable shortening
¾ cup granulated sugar
1 teaspoon baking powder
⅛ teaspoon salt
1 egg
1½ teaspoons vanilla extract
2 cups all-purpose flour

1. *Make the "pizza":* In a large mixing bowl, with an electric mixer set on medium speed, beat the butter and shortening for 1 minute. Add the granulated sugar, baking powder, and salt. Beat for 1 minute. Add the egg and the vanilla, then 1 cup of the flour. Beat for 2 minutes. Add the remaining flour and stir vigorously with a wooden spoon. Wrap the dough in plastic and chill for 15 minutes.

2. Preheat the oven to 375°F. Spread the dough evenly to fit an ungreased 12-inch pizza pan. Bake for 15 to 18 minutes or until the top is golden. Cool in the pan.

3. *Make the topping:* In a medium mixing bowl, combine the chips and the butter. Heat in the microwave oven on Medium for 1 minute and stir. If mixture hasn't melted, return to the microwave and heat in 30-second intervals, stirring after each, until thoroughly melted. Cool for 10 minutes.

For the topping:
½ cup semisweet
  chocolate chips
4 tablespoons (½ stick)
  butter
¼ cup sour cream
1¼ to 1½ cups
  confectioners' sugar
½ cup chopped peanuts

4. With an electric mixer set on medium speed, beat in the sour cream. Add 1¼ cups of the confectioners' sugar and beat until mixture is smooth and easy to spread. Beat in additional sugar as needed to make topping spreadable.

5. Spread topping over the pizza. Sprinkle evenly with chopped peanuts. Cut into wedges when cool.

Sweet Potato and Coconut Pudding

SERVES 6–8

This delicious pudding makes a great dessert—or a sweet side dish to accompany a main course. You can make this ahead of time and reheat it.

Butter for greasing the
  pan
2 pounds sweet potatoes
2 apples
⅔ cup maple-flavored
  pancake syrup
¼ cup (½ stick) melted
  butter
½ teaspoon salt
⅔ cup sweetened flaked
  coconut

1. Preheat the oven to 350°F. Lightly butter a 9 by 13-inch baking pan.

2. Peel sweet potatoes and cut them into chunks. In a large pot of boiling, salted water, cook the potatoes for 10 to 15 minutes or until tender. Drain well. Mash them slightly and set aside.

3. Peel and core the apples; cut them into thin slices.

4. In the prepared baking pan, spread the cooked sweet potatoes in a single layer. Top with the apples.

5. In a small bowl, stir together the syrup, melted butter, and salt. Pour mixture over the sweet potatoes and apples. Sprinkle with the coconut. Bake, uncovered, for 25 to 30 minutes. When the apples are tender, remove from the oven and serve hot.

Sweet-Potato Pie

SERVES 6–8

If you like pumpkin pie, you will love this sweet, creamy dessert. Be sure to keep any leftovers in the refrigerator.

1 recipe Basic Pie Dough
for a 9-inch pie shell
(see page 199)
2 pounds sweet potatoes
¾ cup sugar
2 eggs
1 teaspoon ground
nutmeg
1 teaspoon ground
ginger
½ teaspoon ground
cinnamon
1 teaspoon vanilla
extract
2 tablespoons melted
butter
1½ cups evaporated milk
Whipped cream
(optional)

1. Preheat the oven to 450°F. Line a 9-inch pie pan with the pie dough. Prick it in several places with a fork and place a piece of foil over the pie shell. Bake for 5 minutes. Remove the foil and bake pie shell for another 5 minutes. Remove the pan from the oven.

2. While the pie shell is baking, peel the sweet potatoes and cut them into chunks. In a large pot of boiling, salted water, cook the potatoes for 10 to 15 minutes or until tender. Drain and allow to cool slightly. Mash the potatoes with a potato masher.

3. In a mixing bowl, with an electric mixer set on medium speed, beat the sweet potatoes with the sugar. Beat in the eggs. Add the nutmeg, ginger, cinnamon, and vanilla and beat for 30 seconds. Add the melted butter and the evaporated milk and beat until creamy, about 1 minute. Pour the mixture into the prepared pie shell.

4. Bake the pie for 15 minutes. Reduce the oven temperature to 300°F and continue to bake the pie for 35 to 40 more minutes. When the filling is firm around the edges when you gently jiggle the pie, it is done. Remove from the oven and allow to cool. Serve with whipped cream, if desired.

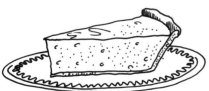

Benne Cakes

MAKES 2 DOZEN

In West Africa, where these cakes are popular, benne means "sesame seeds," and they are eaten for good luck. These sweet cakes are also popular in the American South. They're thin, crisp, and delicious with a glass of milk.

Oil for greasing the
  baking sheet
I cup sesame seeds
I egg
I cup firmly packed
  brown sugar
¼ cup (½ stick) butter,
  at room temperature
I teaspoon vanilla
  extract
I teaspoon freshly
  squeezed lemon juice
¾ cup all-purpose flour
½ teaspoon baking
  powder
¼ teaspoon salt

1. Preheat the oven to 350°F. Lightly oil a baking sheet.

2. Arrange the sesame seeds on a second ungreased baking sheet and place in the oven for 7 to 10 minutes, stirring the seeds occasionally. Remove from the oven and set aside to cool.

3. In a small bowl, lightly beat the egg with a whisk or a fork. In a medium mixing bowl, with an electric mixer set on medium speed, beat the brown sugar with the butter for 2 minutes or until creamy. Add the beaten egg, vanilla, and lemon juice. Beat for 30 seconds.

4. Into a small bowl, sift the flour, baking powder, and salt. Sift the flour mixture into the egg mixture and stir to combine. Stir in the sesame seeds.

5. Drop the dough by rounded teaspoonsful 2 inches apart onto the prepared baking sheet as they will spread. Bake for 15 minutes, until the cookies are lightly browned. Remove the pans from the oven. Remove the cookies from the baking sheet with a spatula. Cool completely on a rack. They are quite thin and fragile when they first come out of the oven but they'll firm up as they cool.

FOR GOODLUCK!

Coconut Custard Pie

If you are just developing a taste for coconut, this is a good pie to try because the flavor isn't overpowering. It tastes like a creamy pudding in a pie crust.

¼ cup (½ stick) butter, at room temperature

¾ cup sugar

3 eggs

1 cup sweetened flaked coconut

½ cup milk

1 teaspoon vanilla extract

1 unbaked 8-inch pie shell [store-bought or use the Basic Pie Dough recipe (page 199)]

1. Preheat the oven to 350°F.

2. In a mixing bowl, with an electric mixer set on medium speed, cream the butter and sugar for 2 minutes or until light and fluffy. Add the eggs, one at a time, beating for 30 seconds after each addition. Add the coconut, milk, and vanilla. Beat for 30 seconds. Pour into the unbaked pie shell.

3. Bake for 40 minutes, or until a knife inserted near the center of the pie comes out clean. Cool on a rack for 1 hour before serving. Be sure to refrigerate leftovers.

Banana Cake

While this dessert uses ordinary bananas, cooks at Kwanzaa sometimes prepare dishes with plantains, which are large, firm bananas that are very popular in Latin America as well as in parts of Asia, India, and Africa. For the best-tasting cake, use very ripe bananas because they will make the cake taste sweeter.

Butter and flour for
   coating the baking
   pan
½ cup (1 stick) butter,
   at room temperature
1½ cups sugar
2 large ripe bananas
2 eggs
1 teaspoon vanilla
   extract
2 cups cake flour
1 teaspoon baking soda
½ teaspoon salt
½ cup yogurt
Vanilla Icing (see page
   235) or confectioners'
   sugar

1. Preheat the oven to 350°F. Lightly butter and flour a 9-inch square cake pan.

2. In a large mixing bowl, with an electric mixer set on medium speed, cream the butter. Slowly add the sugar. Beat for 2 minutes, until very light.

3. Peel and mash the bananas. Add them to the butter-sugar mixture. Add the eggs and vanilla and beat for about 1 minute.

4. Into a medium bowl, sift the cake flour, baking soda, and salt. Add the flour mixture to the butter-sugar mixture and beat on medium speed for 2 minutes. Add the yogurt in 3 parts, beating well after each addition. Spoon and scrape the batter into the prepared pan.

5. Bake for 35 to 45 minutes, until the center of the cake springs back when you touch it with your finger. Cool the cake in the pan.

6. Frost with Vanilla Icing or simply sprinkle with confectioners' sugar.

Index